BEER SOUP FOR THE HASHER'S SOLES

THE HASH HOUSE HARRIERS' GUIDEBOOK

by "Humper"

ON ON

ISBN 978-0-9845957-1-6

First Printing – November 2010
Printed in the United States of America

www.AllAmericanBooks.com

According to Webster:

Hash House (slang), n., a cheap restaurant.

Harrier, n., 1. Any of an English breed of dog used for hunting rabbits. 2. A cross-country runner.

"If you have half a mind to go Hashing... that's all you'll need!"

For
Gator Snapper
The fairest of Harrierettes
&
Move Over Rover
You went On-Out way too soon...

OUR LAGER

(Hasher's Prayer)

Our Lager
Which art in barrels,
Hallowed be thy drink.
Thy will be drunk,
I will be drunk,
At home as in the tavern.
Give us this day our foamy head,
And forgive us our spillages,
As we forgive those who spill against us.
And lead us not into incarceration,
But deliver us from hangovers.
For thine is the Beer, the Bitter, and the Lager,

Barmen!

PREFACE

The Hash House Harriers (abbreviated HHH, H3, or referred to simply as Hashing) is an international group of non-competitive running, social and drinking clubs. An event organized by a club is known as a Hash or Hash Run, with participants calling themselves Hashers.

Variously described as "the lunatic fringe of running" and "the drinking club with a running problem," the Hash House Harriers are a worldwide group with some 350 chapters in the United States and 1700 around the world.

The premise is simple - one Harrier (the Hare) lays a trail of flour over a course (s)he chooses. The other Harriers (the Hounds) try to follow that trail to the end where we enjoy munchies and beer (or soft drinks for those disinclined to imbibe). The typical Hash is 3-5 miles over hill and dale, through suburbs, woods, malls, et al. The Hash isn't a race – there are no prizes to the swift. Following the trail is the challenge, camaraderie and beverages are the rewards.

This book is not intended to be the final word on Hashing, but rather an introduction for the curious, a guide for the newbie, and a source of amusement for the Hasher. The first Rule of Hashing is there are NO rules in Hashing, so nothing set forth herein is set in stone. No two Hashes are alike – they all have their own traditions and peculiarities – and in that uniqueness lies one of the great beauties *of* the Hash!

CONTENTS

Beer Soup For the Hasher's Soles

HASHTORY

A. S. ('G') Gispert

Hashing originated in Kuala Lumpur, Malaysia in 1938 when a group of British colonial officers and expatriates began meeting on Monday evenings to run in a fashion patterned after the traditional British Paper Chase or "Hare and Hounds" to rid themselves of the excesses of the previous weekend. The original members included Cecil Lee, Frederick "Horse" Thomson, Ronald "Torch" Bennett, Albert Stephen "G" Gispert and John Woodrow.

May 23, 1874]   HARE AND HOUNDS   HARPER'S WEEKLY   44]

After meeting for some months, they were informed by the Registrar of Societies that as a "group," they would require a Constitution and an official name. Gispert suggested the name "Hash House Harriers" after the

Selangor Club Annex where the men were billeted, which was known as the "Hash House" for its notoriously monotonous food. Apart from the excitement of chasing the Hare and finding the trail, Harriers reaching the end would be rewarded with beer, ginger beer and cigarettes.

The Constitution of the Hash House Harriers is recorded on a club registration card dated 1950:

- ✓ To promote physical fitness among members.
- ✓ To get rid of weekend hangovers.
- ✓ To acquire a good thirst and to satisfy it in beer.
- ✓ To persuade older members they are not as old as they feel.

Hashing died out during World War II after the invasion of Malaysia, but was re-started after the war by most of the original group minus A. S. Gispert, who was killed in the Japanese invasion of Singapore.

Apart from a "one-off" chapter formed on the Italian Riviera, the growth of Hashing remained small until 1962 when Ian Cumming founded the second kennel in Singapore. The idea then spread through the Far East, Europe, Australia, New Zealand and North America, and began booming in popularity during the mid-1970s.

At present there are almost two thousand kennels in all parts of the world, with members distributing newsletters, directories, and magazines and organizing regional and world Hashing events. As of 2003 there were even two organized kennels operating in Antarctica.

The Original Hash House (Kuala Lumpur) Circa 1938

As previously mentioned, the "Hash House" was the mildly derogative nickname given (for its unimaginative, monotonous food) to the Selangor Club Chambers by the British Civil Servants and businessmen who lived and dined there. The ground floor originally housed the main Selangor Club dining room and between the two World Wars it became a social center of the times, used regularly for lunch time meals by the members who worked in the immediate vicinity.

Situated close to and behind the present Selangor Club, its function changed after independence and it became a key office for the local Water Board, as it was the place where all Kuala Lumpur (K.L.) residents came to pay their water bills. Sadly, it gave way to the relentless march of time around 1964 and was bulldozed to the ground under the north-bound lane of the Jalan Kuching. The buildings housing the original stables and servants quarters are still in existence.

The idea of Harriers chasing paper was not new to Malaya

in 1938, as there had been such clubs before in Kuala Lumpur and and there were clubs in existence in Malacca and Ipoh (the Kinta Harriers) at the time. "Horse" Thomson (one of the KLH3 founding fathers) recalled being invited on a run shortly after his arrival in Johore Bahru in 1932 which chased a paper trail and followed basic Hash rules every week - but was so magically organized that it had no name. The club flourished in the early 1930s, but is believed to have died out around 1935.

The other branch of Hashing ancestry comes from Malacca, where A. S. ('G') Gispert was posted in 1937 and joined a club called the Springgit Harriers who also operated weekly under Hash rules and are believed to have been formed in 1935. Some months later "Torch" Bennett visited him and came as a guest on a few runs.

By 1938 Thomson, Lee, and Gispert had all moved to K.L. and founded their own club, following the rules they had learned elsewhere. The principal original members were all British, although Gispert was actually Spanish in origin, his parents having migrated to London some time before he was born. Extraordinarily, both he and Bennett were accountants - as were Paul Barnard and Jack Bridewell, who made a significant contribution to Hash activities in later years. Some Hash psychiatrist should investigate whether that sort of work leads to extreme forms of escapism!

"Torch" Bennett technically missed being a founding member because he was then on leave, but on his return he introduced the first necessary organization - a bank account, a balance sheet and some sort of system. More importantly,

17

along with Philip Wickens - who joined later in 1939 - he helped to keep things going immediately after the war. The HHH celebrated its 100th run on 15 August 1941, but only seventeen runs later was forced into temporary hibernation by the arrival of the Japanese. Sadly, Gispert had only a short time with his extraordinary creation, being killed in the fighting on Singapore Island on February 11th, 1942 while serving with the Argylls.

Post World War II, it was nearly twelve months before the survivors reassembled. "Torch" Bennett put in a claim for the lost Hash mugs, a tin bath and two old bags, and with the fund set up with the proceeds from confiscated Japanese property the run first run was a trot around the racecourse in August of 1946. Subsequent to the 1,000th post war run the celebrations surrounding it were considered to be such a success that the 117 official pre-war runs were added to the total so the "Mother Hash" could celebrate the 2,000th run as soon as possible.

With the advent of the "Emergency" in 1948 the Hash was automatically in bad official favor, as their activities were generally illegal in terms of the curfew imposed on most of the areas surrounding Kuala Lumpur - and in the years 1948-51 they maintained a precarious existence at best. The turnaround came with the famous bandit incident at Cheras.

This episode has been widely misreported, but what actually happened was that below where the Lady Templer Hospital is now, in an area which then consisted of rubber and belukar, the Hares one dark and rainy evening came across some men wrapped in sheets sleeping on the ground.

The following pack found the bandits on their feet, but somehow in the general confusion nobody got hurt. One member ran to Cheras Police Station and raised the alarm, and the army laid ambushes on tracks leading out of the area. The first thing the following morning they bagged three bandits trying to break out, and when one of them was found to have a substantial price on his head the bounty was shared amongst the non-government employees on the run (since government servants were not allowed to participate in such rewards).

Other colorful incidents related by Cecil Lee include how "Torch" Bennett once nearly drowned in quicksand and how on one memorable occasion the erstwhile unathletic 'G' was actually leading the pack – but sadly his moment of glory was short-lived when the trail turned out to be false. Swimming would seem to be an unofficial prerequisite for all Hashers too, for Cecil remembers having to swim across a mining pool in order to get home after being lost on one occasion, and on another it is reported that several Hashers ran into a stream where some unsuspecting Malaysian maidens were bathing. The girls screamed, their menfolk came hurtling to the rescue with the unsheathed parangs flashing, and the errant Hashers broke all sorts of land speed records in their eagerness to clear the scene.

The second Hash chapter was founded in Singapore in 1962, followed by Kuching in 1963, Brunei, Kota Kinabalu and Ipoh in 1964, and Penang in 1965. Perth, Australia was the first outside Malaysia, and followed in 1967. Even by the time of K.L. 1,500th run in 1974 the total was only thirty-five, so the subsequent explosion has been spectacular indeed. The 1992 international list totaled around 1,100 clubs in over 135 countries and on all seven continents (including Antarctica) where the Hash format is often adapted to environments very different from the Malaysian rubber trees amongst which it was conceived. Kabul HHH understandably foundered, but what must it be like to Hash in Sinai, Peking, Addis Ababa or the Falkland Islands?

The first attempts at an Interhash get-together were the K.L. 1,000th post-war run in 1966, and the spectacular 1500th run in 1973 when attendance was something over 300. Interhash 1978 in Hong Kong broke new ground with an attendance of around 800, Interhashes 1980 and 1982 were credited with 1,300, Interhash 1986 broke the 2,000 barrier, and such events have grown exponentially from there in recent years.

HASH FACT

Many Hashes around the world now celebrate 'G's birthday on July 31st, or the anniversary of his death on February 11th. The original, and most significant, event is the annual run from the Singapore War Cemetery at Kranji on the nearest Sunday to February 11th.

HASHING

Although the Hash is often called a "drinking club with a running problem," many Hashers are actually teetoatlers!

The Hash House Harriers is a decentralized organization with each chapter (sometimes called a kennel) individually managed with no uniting organizational hierarchy (although the locations of national and international gatherings are decided by a meeting involving representatives from a number of Hashes). A kennel's management is typically known as the "Mis-Management," and consists of individuals with various duties and titles. There are more than 1,700 kennels spanning all seven continents, and most major cities are home to at least one chapter. Kennels typically contain 20-100 members, usually mixed-sex, and some metropolitan area Hashes can draw more than a thousand Hashers to an event.

Most kennels gather on a weekly or monthly basis, though some events occur sporadically, e.g. February 29th, Friday the 13th, or a full moon. Generally, Hash events are open to the public and require no reservation or membership, and usually require a small fee, referred to as "hashcash," to cover the costs incurred such as food or drink. As previously noted members often describe their group as "a drinking club with a running problem," indicating that the social element of an event is as important, if not more so, than any athleticism involved. Beer remains an integral part of a Hash, though the balance between running and drinking differs between kennels with some groups placing more focus on socializing and others on running.

At a Hash one or more members (Hares) lay a trail, which is then followed by the remainder of the group (the Pack or Hounds). The trail often includes false trails, short cuts, dead ends, and splits. These features are designed to keep the pack together regardless of fitness level or running speed, as front-runners are forced to slow down to find the "true" trail, allowing stragglers to catch up.

Hashing hasn't strayed far from its roots in Kuala Lumpur. The Hare(s) mark their trail with paper, chalk, sawdust or colored flour, depending on the environment and weather. Special marks may be used to indicate a false trail, a backtrack, a shortcut or a turn. The most commonly-used mark is a "check," indicating that Hashers will have to search in any direction to find the continuation of the trail. Trails may also contain a "beer check," where the pack stops to consume beer, water or snacks and any stragglers can catch up to the pack.

Trails may pass through any sort of terrain and Hashers may run through back alleyways, residential areas, city streets, forests, swamps or shopping malls and may climb fences, ford streams, explore storm drains or scale cliffs in their pursuit of the Hare.

There are two types of trails, "live" and "dead." Live trails are laid by Hares who are given a head start, while dead trails are pre-laid hours or days before the Hash begins. Live trails and dead trails are also known as "live Hare" and "dead Hare" trails, respectively. Live trails are closer to the original "Hare and Hound" tradition, with the object being the pack catching the Hare rather than simply making it to the end. This type is more common in the United States, while the rest of the world tends toward dead trails.

A trail may be "A to A," where the trail returns to the

start, or "A to B," where the beginning and end of the trail are widely separated. Some trails are also referred to as "A to A1," denoting an ending point that is close to, but not the same as, the start.

While following trail Hashers shout "On-on!" when they see markings, and some Hashers carry horns or whistles to signal to one another in addition to verbal communication. Every Hash employs its own set of marks and the names for these marks may vary widely, so newcomers or visitors will have the local markings explained to them before the run at a "chalk talk." Additionally, the Hares for that particular run may give some trail-specific advice, such as rare markings or particular obstacles.

Most Hash events end with a group gathering known as the "circle," or less commonly, "religion." Led by kennel leadership (usually the Religious Advisor), the circle provides a time to socialize, sing drinking songs, recognize individuals, formally name members, inform the group of pertinent news or upcoming events, and perform "down downs."

A down-down is a means of punishing, rewarding or merely recognizing an individual for any action or behavior according to the customs or whims of the group. Generally, the individual in question is asked to consume without pause the contents of his or her drinking vessel or pour the remaining contents on his or her head, i.e. "That which does not go in you, goes on you!" Individuals may be recognized for outstanding service, or for their status as a visitor or newcomer. Down-downs also serve as punishment for misdemeanors, whether they be real, imagined or blatantly made up. Such transgressions may include failing to stop at the beer check, pointing with a finger (elbows should be used, because a good Hasher always has a drinking vessel in his or her hand!), or the use of real names.

A special type of down-down is often reserved for Hashers who wear new shoes to the Hash. The Hasher is required to remove one shoe, which is then filled with beer and serves as the vessel for the down-down – and in some kennels the beer is further filtered through the accused's sweaty sock.

Many kennels include an ice seat or throne as part of the ceremony. Those who are to consume a down-down sit on a large block of ice while they await the completion of the down-down song... and if the offense which resulted in the down-down is particularly egregious, the Hasher may be subjected to a long song with many verses. In some kennels the Hasher must remove any attire that comes between his/her seat and the ice, while others allow errant Hashers to keep their underwear on but require the outer garments to be removed.

While the circle at the end of a trail is an opportunity to socialize, have a drink and observe any traditions of the individual kennel, once the Hash officially ends many members may continue socializing at an "On-After" or "On-On-On," an event held at a nearby house, pub or restaurant.

In most kennels, the use of real names during an event is discouraged. Members are typically given a "Hash name," usually in recognition of a particularly notorious escapade, a personality trait or their physical appearance. In some kennels the name must be earned - that is, Hashers are not named until they've done something outstanding, unusual or stupid enough to *warrant* a name. In other kennels the process is more mechanical, and Hashers are named after completing a certain number of runs (with 5-10 being the most common).

Some kennels prefer "family-friendly" names (for example, "Lost My Way"), while others focus on names filled with innuendo (for example, "Salt Lick"). Still others go out of their way to make the name as bawdy, scatological, offensive and/or politically incorrect as possible (no example given because these names are limited only by the imagination of the kennel).

Those Hashers who have not yet been named are generally referred to as "Just (Name)," e.g. "Just Dave," or "No Fucking Hash Name (Name)," e.g. "No Fucking Hash Name Jessica," with *first time* Hashers being known as "Virgin (Name)."

Hashers are *not* permitted to give themselves nicknames due to the obvious conflict of interest, and those who do so are often renamed by the kennel at the earliest opportunity with a far more offensive name. Similarly, Hashers who do get named and don't like their new moniker may end up being renamed by their kennel – and the members will no doubt strive to give the complaining Hasher an even more objectionable or inappropriate name.

In addition to regularly-scheduled Hashes, a kennel may also organize other events or themed runs. A common special event is the Red Dress Run, which is held annually by individual kennels. According to Hash lore, a newcomer in San Diego was invited to a Hash. Unbeknownst to her it was a running group, and she attended the run in a red dress instead of running clothes. After being mocked for wearing such an outfit she ran the trail anyway, and other Hashers began wearing red dresses as a joke and the tradition soon became an annual event which spread around the world. The point of the run is all participants (of both sexes) don red dresses of various sorts. The Red Dress is typically the largest event organized by a kennel in a given year with attendance topping 2,000 in San Diego and 600 in Washington, D.C., with the largest in New Orleans with approximately 5000 participants. Red Dress Runs are traditionally used as charity fundraisers, although the Hash itself is not per se a charitable body.

There are also a number of variations on the traditional Hash concept. Bicycle Hashes ("Bashes") follow normal Hashing traditions with the Hare and pack riding bicycles, and Family Hashes welcome children (sometimes called "Hash House Horrors") with soft drinks replacing alcoholic beverages and drinking songs toned down appropriately.

HASH FACT

Although the Singapore Hash is widely credited with being the second one formed, the Royal Italian Bordighera Hash was begun in 1947 but died out by the late '50s. It was later resurrected by members of the Milan Hash and became popular in the mid '70s.

"JOBS"

Like any other club or organization, it takes the efforts of a few dedicated individuals to keep the Hash "running."

BEERMEISTER: This is unquestionably the most important position in the Hash. The Beermeister has the weighty responsibility of making sure the lifeblood of Hashing is available at each and every Hash event. He keeps constant vigilance to find the cheapest "spirituous fermenti" available, always has coolers in the trunk of his car and cases of beer in his garage, and reliably returns the empty keg between the On-On and On-On-On. This job requires a strong back, and a weak mind!

GRAND MASTER: The head man. The chairman of the board. The big cheese. The HMFIC. The guiding light. Gispert's legacy. The GM is not simply a figurehead for the Hash, but rather he (or she) personifies the Hash's character (or lack thereof.) He leads with a dynamic strength that permeates the fabric of the organization. Both directly, and through his officers, he gives inspiration, direction and vision to all. This position ranks only below Beermeister, Hash Cash, Hash Mouth, and Hash Flash in real importance to the Hash.

HABADASHER Seller and often procurer and designer of Hash gear. Often seems to be a mythical creature, i.e. when you are visiting another Hash you always seem to hear, "This is the first run he has missed in three years!"

HARE RAISER: The Hare Raiser makes sure that there's a Hare (or Hares) for each Hash, and that the start location is known to the On-Sec well in advance of Hash day for publicity purposes. The Hare Raiser IS the Hare if (s)he can't find anyone else to do it – which provides ample motivation to do a proper job!

HASH CASH: The holder of the purse-strings. Someone needs to dash about the start of each Hash begging for money. Someone has to keep track of what comes in and what goes out (commonly referred to as "the old in and out.") These generally unappreciated duties fall on the shoulders of the Hash Cash. This trustworthy soul must withstand the whining of the Hares who have over-spent, the whimpering of those who have forgotten their fees, and the interrogations of those who mistakenly think there should be some sort of accounting for Hash funds. The Hash Cash sometimes also acts as Hash Haberdasher, procuring and selling items of apparel to the Hash.

HASH FLASH: The person who captures on film for posterity all embarrassing Hash moments. The Hash Flash must have an acute sense of the absurd to know what to take photos of, and also a small degree of reliability to bring a camera, film, take pictures, have them developed (or in the case of digital photos, uploaded), and put only the finest thereof onto the web or into the sacred photo album.

HASH HARLOT: A trashy wench who has seen the dark side of Hashing, and likes it! One with a lust for life who revels in being the butt of the jester's ribald wit, the object of the songmeister's bawdy lyric, and the centerpiece of all sensual Hash repartee. (AKA "Hash Mattress")

HASH HORN: Equipment requirements: A bugle or other appropriate wind instrument. Performance venue: The Hash trail. Musical ability: Optional. This position is more common in Commonwealth countries than in the United States.

HASH MATTRESS: Provides a place for visiting out-of-town Hashers to crash. Alternately, see "Hash Harlot."

HASH MOUTH: The Hash Mouth runs the official business at the On-On with an iron hand. He must be loud, clear, passionate, articulate, humorous and possess an uncommon ability to think on his feet. It also helps if he speaks English.

HASHIT KEEPER: This is arguably the most complicated position within the Hash hierarchy. The responsibility surrounds custody of a large cardboard box filled with the flotsam and jetsam of past Hashes. Precisely why this crap is retained is a mystery shrouded in the mythology of Hashdom, however the Hashit itself rarely makes it to the Hash - although the custodian is almost always there himself. This reinforces the argument that remembering to bring the Hashit is probably beyond the cognitive ability of your average Hasher.

HASH TRASH: Produces the weekly or monthly newsletter published within a kennel. The idea started in KL sometime in the early years, with the oldest surviving copy being produced for the 100th run. The Hash Trash gives details of the next Hash, and contains a report of the previous run.

ON-SEC: This position is the masochist's dream. He struggles with piles of papers, miles of computer wire, and helps produce a Hash Trash to keep the Hash members reasonably informed. He is the official representative on the Internet - maintaining the Website, email lists and other such forms of nonsense. The On-Sec also maintains the Hash membership data base and publishes the Hound Directory. Boring stuff to say the least!

ROAD WHORE: Plans and coordinates group road trips to visit other Hashes or attend debaucherous and hedonistic events such as Interhash and Nash Hash.

SONGMEISTER: This is a Hasher with no self-respect who never lacks for a song suitable to the occasion. His songs are risqué, lewd and vulgar. The Songmeister speaks with other Hashers and Hashes to acquire new songs to add to the Hash Hymnal. The mission is to explore new tunes and new celebrations. To boldly go where no Songmeister has gone before (pardon the split infinitive.)

RELIGIOUS ADVISOR: Keeper of the Faith. Enforcer of the Scriptures. This is the Hasher who has seen the light (often *Bud Light*) and can taste in his soul the true spirit of Hashing. The Religious Advisor spreads the word and inspires the zest and zeal of the Hash in all participants. Any Hasher found transgressing the spirit of Hashing is disciplined by the RA. He is the keeper of the sacred Laws of Hashing - and comes up with sufficiently plausible lies to cover any serious questions of propriety.

HASH FACT

A Harrier is related to the Foxhound and bred specifically for chasing rabbits or hares. Hence the Hare sets the trail and the pack of Harriers follows it.

HARING

Haring is the most important responsibility that can be entrusted to a Hasher- so it's important to do it right!

Haring is without question the most important responsibility that can be entrusted to a Hasher, and it takes planning, insight, and creativity to lay an exciting trail and establish the conditions for a great On-In afterward.

Every Hash has a few wallflowers - Harriers and Harrierttes who show up every week but never *ever* Hare. You can beg, plead, and threaten… but they always have an excuse. I suspect that when you get right down to it, the really determined wallflower is *afraid* to Hare. Afraid of doing something for the first time, afraid of being criticized for messing up the trail, afraid of being compared with better Hares - and in a live Hare Hash, afraid of getting caught! What they don't realize is even seasoned Hares experience some sort of pre-trail anxiety. It comes with the territory, and it's part of the thrill of Haring.

Haring is uniquely rewarding. It really is a kick to plan a trail, especially if you've discovered some unexplored, challenging terrain to spice it up, and there are so many possibilities - long straight A to Bs, eagle/turkey splits, uphill detours begging to be BTs, circular trails that can either be A to As, A to almost-As, and even A to Bs. Few things in life rise to the level of satisfaction you'll get from finishing your trail and then running back to a vantage point where you can watch the pack finding their way on-in - except perhaps the pleasure of knowing you finished your trail without getting caught! Yes, it's rewarding. It adds a new dimension to your enjoyment of Hashing, and once you've tried it you'll want to do it again.

For the benefit of experienced Hares who want to learn

more about the art, for novice Hares giving it a go for the first time, and especially for Hashers who would sign up to Hare if they didn't find the whole deal so intimidating, here are some tips and techniques:

Get On the Schedule

If you want to Hare (and you should) you first need to coordinate with the Hare Raiser to get on the schedule. The "Receding Hare Line" is usually filled six or more months in advance, so plan ahead to get the date you want (such as near your birthday for you narcissistic types). Many Hashes utilize the internet these days, so you can simply check the online schedule to see which dates are available.

A note for Virgin (first time) Hares - you must have a veteran Co-Hare! There's no substitute for experience, and you can learn much from your grizzled old partner. If you don't arrange for a suitably experienced Co-Hare yourself, the Hare Raiser will appoint one for you.

Planning the Hash

The first thing you should establish is the type of Hash. You have two choices, dead Hare or live Hare:

Dead Hare is where the entire trail is laid a few hours before the start of the Hash, with the rationale being it provides the opportunity for people of all athletic abilities to lay trail and also allows time to construct a more elaborate system of checks.

Many people, however, like live trails because of the additional element of suspense wherein the Hares might be caught. In a live Hare environment, the Hares are given a fifteen minute head start and lay the trail in real time. They do their best to provide a good trail, while at the same time trying to avoid being caught by the Hounds. If caught the Hare might briefly loose his or her pants, and the "catcher" might become a Co-Hare from that point on.

The On-Before

The On-Before at a bar is a traditional part of the Hash experience in many kennels. It's the Hare's responsibility to:

- ✓ Find a suitable On-Before location.

- ✓ Make it as close to the start as practical.

- ✓ Coordinate with the bar management. Try to get special prices, but at the very least let them know that for an hour or so there'll be an additional fifty patrons.

Plan for Bad Weather

More than once Hashes have ended on a hilltop during a thunderstorm without choice, therefore you should have an alternate indoor location in mind. Also think about shortcuts for really bad weather, or even calling off a part of the trail when the weather is too bad.

Theme Hashes

While not required, themed Hashes can be fun. Some traditional theme Hashes include Mardi Gras, Red Dress and Jingle Balls. For your Hash, try to come up with something new and appropriate. Some examples are having Hashers put on clothing left at checks, or hiding stuff around checks as part of a scavenger hunt - you get the idea. Use your imagination. One caveat... if you encourage Hashers to wear costumes and then take them through costume-shredding shiggy, they will revolt. The best costume Hashes are run in high visibility areas.

Birthdays

It's common for Hashers to Hare a trail on their birthday, but let's be frank, birthdays are not all that unusual - everyone has one per year. Therefore, you might want to consider a theme other than a celebration of yourself.

Coordination

Let the Beermeister know what kind of beer support you'll need. If you plan on having a beer check and the end is in your back yard, the beer requirement is far different than if there's no beer check and the end is at a public establishment.

It's the Hare's responsibility to contact the Beermeister,

preferably a few weeks out, but certainly not later than one week before the Hash. He'll need to know whether you need a keg (and where it should be delivered), if you are going with cans, and whether or not there'll be a beer check. Please be considerate of the Beermeister. He's got the worst - but most important - job in the Hash. Don't force him to chase you down to find out what your beer needs are.

If the On-In is at a bar, inform the Hash Cash at the start of the Hash to arrange for a transfer of funds to pay for beer at the establishment.

You can swap dates with another Hare, but you must let the Hare Raiser know. This is not to obtain permission, but simply to keep the attending confusion to the minimum.

🦶 Money Matters

Capitalized, the term "Hash Cash" refers to the person who manages the financial resources of the kennel. When written in lower case, "hash cash" represents the actual financial resources (i.e., the money you must fork over).

It's important for Hares understand the use of hash cash and not unknowingly undertake expenditures which are not reimbursable - if in fact your Hash requires the Hare to handle such things, and does not delegate these responsibilities to a member of Mis-Management.

The Hash Cash collects $5.00 (or whatever is appropriate for your kennel) from each Hasher per Hash, with the exception that Virgins (first time Hashers) and Hares do not pay. The reason Hares do not pay is they encounter expenses which Hounds do not such as flour, chalk and flyer creation/reproduction - so please do not seek special reimbursement for these incidental expenses. Free beer also serves as a great incentive for wallflowers to get out there and lay a trail!

Of the money collected from paying Hashers, most is used to pay for beer, soft drinks, ice and munchies and the rest is usually retained in the Hash "superfund" for contingencies and emergencies.

For each Hash that does not end at a public establishment, the Hash Cash will fully reimburse the Beermeister for one keg of beer or the amount of canned beer consumed, plus soft drinks and ice. Any remaining monies can be used to pay for munchies (chips and dips and the like).

For Hashes which end at a public establishment, the Hash Cash will provide the Hare a predetermined amount per person to spend at the bar. The Hash will not pay for unlimited beer - it is up to the Hare to negotiate reasonable prices, and to make financial settlement with the establishment. And please don't forget to figure in the serving staff's gratuity!

Once the Hash's cash is exhausted, the Hares can buy additional beer at their personal expense or "pass the hat" for donations to keep the beer flowing. Another option is to go "every wanker for himself" from that point.

At this point it is a good idea to discuss the quality of beer usually purchased. To stretch the Hash's cash as far as possible, the Beermeister's selection of beer is usually rather pedestrian (that means cheap!). If the Hares wish they may of course supply higher quality (homebrew, microbrew, commercial premium) beer themselves, however reimbursement will only be at the rate of an equivalent amount of the normal cheap beer. For example, if the Hares buy a keg of Fat Tire Ale for $110, the Hash Cash will only reimburse them for the going price of a keg of Busch or its equivalent (probably around $50.00).

Publicity

Once you have committed to Haring it's often a good idea to create a flyer and pass out copies at the Hash immediately preceding yours – although with the advent of the internet online "flyers" are usually preferred in developed countries. Either way, the elements of essential information to be included are:

WHAT: (Hash #???)
WHEN: (Month, Day, Year, Time)
WHERE: (Start location)
HARES: (Your names)
THEME: (If any)
TRAIL: (Length and Difficulty)
DOG FRIENDLY: (Yes/No)
ON-BEFORE: (Location)
BRING: (Amount of hash cash, whistle, flashlight, etc.)
DIRECTIONS: (Important!)

Planning the Trail

Scout your trail early and often. This means actually running and/or walking it several times to get a good feel for its viability in terms of length, difficulty (shiggy) and opportunities for pleasant surprises. You can't scout a good trail from a car or off a topographical map, but both can be useful support items. Just don't cross private land without permission!

Trail should normally be in the three to five mile range, but certainly never more than six miles or so. Evaluate your trail in terms of length, and rate it in difficulty.

Once you've evaluated the trail, use the description in the publicity campaign for your Hash. This is a simple courtesy to give the Hounds some idea of what they're up against and can serve to head off later complaints about the trail.

Plan for a "shag vehicle" to get baggage to the end if it is an A to B trail, and to the beer check on cold or rainy days. If you need help, enlist the assistance of an Auto Hasher.

Finally, don't use the Hash to demonstrate your superb physical fitness. The point of the Hash is for both Hares and Hounds to have fun – and as a Hound, getting your dick knocked into the dirt simply isn't fun, no matter how amused the Hare is about it all.

Types of Trail

There are three basic trail configurations: A-to-A, A-to-A+, and A-to-B. If you're a Hasher you know what all that means. If you aren't, here are some short definitions:

- ❖ A-to-A: a trail that starts and ends at the same place.
- ❖ A-to-A+: a trail that ends near the start.
- ❖ A-to-B: a point-to-point trail.

The advantage of laying an A-to-A or A-to-A+ trail is logistical: you don't have to transport beer, snacks, and Hash bags from one place to another, and you don't have to worry about getting Hashers back to the start after the circle. For the pack, the advantage of this type of trail is it's hard to get lost. On an A-to-A trail, you know exactly where you're going (and you can cut back at any time if you're lazy); on an A-to-A+ trail, even if you manage to get lost you can still find the end without too much trouble. Oh, and all your stuff… your warm clothes, your dry shoes, your car… is at or very near the end.

As a Hare, the disadvantage of laying an out-and-back trail is the possibility of getting caught by shortcutters. You can run away from the start and stay ahead of the pack, but at some point you have to start circling back - and that's where they'll nab you. There are really only two ways to lay such a trail without getting caught - be lucky, or cheat.

Luck involves setting a circular trail so wide in diameter that shortcutters would have to be able to predict which direction your circle will take, and then divine exactly where you'll be on the return leg. The trouble with luck is, shortcutters get lucky too.

Cheating involves pre-laying portions of your trail. I'm sorry, there's just no way to say that politely. If you really really don't want to get caught, and you want to lay any sort of out-and-back trail, you're going to have to pre-lay part of it. Usually Hares pre-lay the far side of the circle. This allows them to live-lay the start and the end, cutting out the section they already marked.

Hashers who come from groups with a live-Hare tradition generally don't approve of Hares pre-laying. Hashers who come from groups with a strong shortcutting tradition absolutely *hate* pre-laying. They want to catch Hares - that's why they short-cut! Not that this means much to Hares, who almost universally pre-lay, with varying degrees of stealth and secrecy.

A few Hares, though, are hard core. They are the ones who, when they're not Haring, are the shortcutters who live to *catch* Hares. When these Harriers and Harriettes lay trail, they lay it live with no pre-laying. They are the Hares who gave us the A-to-B trail. Because they are good runners their survival technique is to take off and go balls to the wall, blitzing straight ahead for five to seven miles, and then they stop - and where they stop, that's the end.

As far as Hares are concerned, the advantage of an A-to-B trail is not getting caught. Who can shortcut a straight line? As for the pack, the advantage is the unpredictability of the trail and not knowing where you're going until you get there. It doesn't sound like much, but for some Hashers that's exciting.

The disadvantage of A-to-B trails for Hares is figuring out

how to transport everything the Hash needs for the circle... beer, snacks, and bags... from the start to the end, and doing it while the pack is still on trail so that it's all there waiting for them, and then getting all of that stuff, plus the Hashers themselves, back to the start when the circle's over so that everyone can retrieve their cars and drive to the On-after. It isn't easy.

The disadvantage of A-to-B trails is almost the same for the pack. How do you get back to your car if you need to leave the circle early? Do you walk or run? Even if the Hares have a car at the end (they usually do) they can only shuttle a few Hashers at a time back for cars, so you might have to wait until the first (or even second) carload returns with more cars before there's room for you... and then you get Hashers who take the first ride back to the start but don't come back to transport other Hashers (the selfish bastards!) and there's always a few of those, but that's another subject.

Worldwide, Hashes are divided about fifty-fifty in terms of whether their Hares lay trail live or dead. Dead-Hare Hashes almost always set A-to-A or A-to-A+ trails. Live-Hare Hashes set all types of trail, mostly A-to-A and A-to-A+, but occasionally A-to-B.

Live Hare Trails

Find an experienced co-Hare to help you lay your first live trail, and listen to his or her advice. This really is the best way to learn, and it'll give you added confidence - and you can be sure your co-Hare will help you plan your trail to minimize the chance of getting caught. The following are some live-Hare techniques tailored to different levels of running prowess:

Front Running Bastard

Just go for it. You probably don't even need a co-Hare. All you have to worry about is using up your head start with checks, loops, and bad trails, so be sure to wear a stopwatch and remember to hack it when you take off. Plan a fairly straight A to B and you're in there. If you can't carry enough flour to lay the entire trail, you may want to go out ahead of time and stash an extra bag somewhere on trail.

Head of the Pack Runner

Go out one or two hours early and pre-lay your longer bad trails and loops. This will allow you (and your co-Hare, if you have one) to take maximum advantage of your head start and let you Hare just the basic trail from start to finish. Be very careful if you're laying a circular trail, though - short-cutters might head out backwards and catch you on your way in! Laying an A to B trail is still the best way to avoid getting caught.

Middle of the Pack Runner

Recruit a good runner as co-Hare, and have him or her run the complete trail and lay the middle portion. You lay the first part, then detour off-trail to a place where you can pick up and lay the end. Alternately, have your co-Hare lay the first two-thirds of the trail while you run straight to a point where you can pick up the last third. Both techniques require a circular trail, though not necessarily an A to A.

Back of the Pack Runner

Pre-lay half of your trail, the middle part. Live Hare the first quarter, hide until the pack passes, then detour straight to a point where you can pick up and lay the last quarter. Once again, you'll need a circular trail for this to work. Just make sure you wait for the DFLs to pass before you come out of hiding!

Fat Boy

Pre-lay nine-tenths of your trail. Run the first tenth, then hop in the car you stashed ahead of time (don't forget your keys!) and drive to the end (being sure to park the car out of sight). Trail type no longer matters - you can set it straight or you can set it circular. You can even set a rhomboid if you want!

Keep Up the Pretense

No matter which technique you use, keep the details to yourself and your co-Hares. As far as the pack is concerned, you Hared the entire trail live!

🐾 Regardless of Running Ability

Start planning trail at least a couple of weeks before the event. Pick the area you want to run in, then select start and finish locations. Many Hares pick the finish location first and start planning from there. There are many considerations in picking start and finish locations - parking, shade, places for boys and girls to pee, and a reasonable amount of isolation from civilians so you can sing and drink afterwards. Plan the route from start to finish. Begin with map study, then walk the route. Look for animal or kid trails - they'll lead you to the secret spots where chain link fences have been cut, the best places to cross streams, the best routes up and down cliffs, etc. Pick the best places for checks, and make your BTs convincing. Your trail should keep the FRBs busy solving checks, allowing the pack to catch up. Live run or walk your trail at least once, timing yourself. You should be able to run the basic trail (without taking bad trails) in thirty to forty-five minutes, or walk it in forty-five minutes to an hour. Don't worry that it's too short. With checks, bad trails and loops, the pack will be out for an hour or slightly longer.

🐾 Dead Hare Trails

At first glance, dead-Haring appears easier than live-Haring, but that's not necessarily the case. You should still work with an experienced co-Hare at first. Quite often novice dead-Hares lay overly complicated, way-too-long trails simply because without the worry of getting caught - they *can*. Here are some thoughts on dead-Hare trails:

Plan Ahead

Live or dead, the basics are the same: you need to plan ahead, putting some thought into start and finish locations as well as the route. You still want to lay a trail that will keep the pack together, slowing down the FRBs and allow the slower runners an opportunity to catch up. Overall length should be the same as a live trail. It shouldn't take you much more than an hour to walk your basic trail from start to finish.

The difference between live and dead Haring is you have time to lay a more complex trail, with no pressure to hurry - just don't get carried away! Your only real-time constraint is how early you can pre-lay and still expect your trail to be there when the pack runs it. A rainstorm between your pre-lay and the start of the Hash can be disastrous and undo all your hard work. So can an anal property owner with a broom or garden hose. The point is don't pre-lay trail too early. One to two hours before the start is about the right time to set out with your bag of flour.

It's also easier to take advantage of public transportation when you dead Hare. You can time the start so that the pack, after running the first half-mile for example, will arrive at a bus or subway stop in time to catch a ride to another part of town where trail will resume. Elevators and ferry boats are always a nice touch. Be inventive. Just be sure that if you try this, do it early enough on the trail that the pack is still together and no one gets left behind (and it's up to you as the

Hare to figure out how to pay for special twists like this).

Another consideration is a live Hare who is running is more likely to be challenged and turned away from certain venues than a dead Hare who is discreetly walking and looking innocent. If you traverse fancy malls, hotel pool areas, casinos, train stations, private beaches, gated neighborhoods, or outdoor wedding ceremonies you can certainly set the pack up for some high profile encounters! Obviously a little of this can go a long way, and personally I always think twice about laying trail through areas where the pack is likely to get arrested for trespassing - and then I go ahead and do it anyway!

Finally, as a dead Hare, you should plan to run or walk behind the pack looking for DOTs and helping them get back on trail.

Safety

Remember that not everyone is a rock climber or an Olympic swimmer, so avoid the truly dangerous stuff. Examples include, but are not limited to: culverts during thunderstorm season, dangerous or violent neighborhoods (especially after dark), and any crossing of a major highway at street level.

Turkey trails are supposed to be EASY, not just easier, so that Hashers in less than great physical conditions don't suffer heart attacks on-trail. Include a beer check or "Hash Halt" (regroup) to permit the less athletic (and the lost) time to catch up to the pack.

Beer Checks

Plan the logistics of the beer check carefully. You'll need to get the beer there before the FRBs arrive, and clean up the area after everyone leaves. It should be a place where Hashers can enjoy a beer without getting harassed, so avoid places where a group of 40-50 people drinking will draw undue attention. Out of sight under a bridge or behind a vacant building usually works fairly well.

You can also stash the beer in a cooler or whatever (i.e., an unmanned beer check). If you do this, leave a trash bag for the empties and remember to return and pick it up after the Hash.

In the opinion of some, a beer check on a live-Hared trail is considered an unethical means to avoid getting caught. Nevertheless, it is a perfectly acceptable tactic. Again, if you need help enlist the assistance of an Auto Hasher.

Water (yes, *water!*)

Always have sufficient drinking water available at the beer check. While it's an individual Hasher's responsibility to prevent dehydration (that is, carry a water bottle on trail), there should be a little extra effort to provide water at the beer check. Hashers will use this water to both drink and refill their water bottles, and many people prefer water on trail and defer their beer drinking until the On-In. Others will enjoy a drink of water *and* a brew, and if you say it's a dog friendly trail you should provide enough water for both people and dogs - Fido shouldn't have to drink Schlitz! If you provide water in bulk rather than in bottles, also provide a means for people and animals to drink it. This mean plastic or paper cups.

Dogs

While the Hash certainly isn't a kennel club, a few Hashers want to bring their pets to the run. This practice should be neither encouraged nor discouraged - therefore it's the Hare's responsibility to assess the trail and On-In as to whether or not it's "dog friendly" and include the information in the publicity release. Normally an On-In at a public establishment is unsuitable for dogs, and there are certain trail characteristics which make the presence of dogs impractical (e.g., trails which go through structures such as malls and hotels, water crossings more than knee deep, or transportation like buses or U-Haul vans).

Logistics

Hash-day logistics are quite frankly a pain, but essential to a successful event. The Hare has many logistical responsibilities which, if not carefully planned for, can detract from his ability to lay the trail or result in delays and dry spells at the On-In. While the shag wagon, beer check, ice, keg, etc. are the responsibility of the Hare, that does not mean the Hare must do everything him/herself - and it is perfectly acceptable to enlist the assistance of others to take care of logistical matters. Assistants can come in the form of Auto Hashers, or even Non-Hashers - it really doesn't matter. What *does* matter is that the beer is flowing at the On-In when the Front Running Bastards (FRBs) arrive, and that the shag wagon is nearby and accessible!

Three important things to not to lose sight of:

❖ Actual weather conditions on the day of your Hash can ruin the best laid plans.

❖ Once the Hash starts, it's no longer in your control.

❖ Every Hare has a trail that *will not work*.

Laying the Trail

Before laying the trail, make sure that both you and your Hare partner(s) are all using the same marking conventions. Otherwise you just may confuse the Hounds and get them lost - and into an ugly mood.

Don't screw with the pack by making the trail difficult to find... screw with the pack by where the trail *goes*. It's far better to lay a trail that's easy to find and a son-of-a-bitch to traverse, than vice-versa.

Assigning segments of the trail to different Hares to lay independently is a sure recipe for disaster. The only guaranteed way to ensure a coherent trail is for all Hares to lay the trail together.

Trail Marks

A few tips for marking trail:

- ✓ Use lots of flour. Once again, use *lots* of flour. This can't be emphasized enough. Ideally, Hounds should be able to see the next mark from the last.

- ✓ Hash marks should be placed about twenty-five yards or so apart, and never be more than fifty.

- ✓ When "bushwhacking," make marks very close together.

- ✓ Consider alternate marking when bushwhacking, such as surveyor/engineer tape or toilet paper.

- ✓ Mark your trail with environmentally friendly substances. That means no spray paint, and remember that after the Hash you must remove anything you used that the rain won't easily eradicate (e.g., surveyor/engineer tape).

- ✓ Sidewalk chalk is great... but only when it isn't raining.

- ✓ Don't get *too* clever with your marking medium. Animals just might find certain things irresistible (like Fruit Loops cereal) and eat your marks.

✓ If you change direction, mark the change with either a check or a Hare arrow.

✓ There is no requirement to lay false trails from a check, but there *must* be a true trail.

✓ End your false trails with a false trail mark, especially on pre-laid trails where a "blow job" (false trail without a false trail mark) make little sense.

✓ Three flour marks after a check means true trail. After three Hash marks it is not Kosher to lay a false trail mark. A check (which may include false trails), on the other hand, is quite appropriate.

✓ Not getting caught is a matter of cleverness (and luck), not speed. Don't double back – you're bound to run into a short cutting bastart (SCB). Most live Hares are caught by SCBs, *not* FRBs!

Checks

Checks are critical because they keep packs together and Front Running Bastards (FRBs) confused. Ideally, the Dead Fu*king Last (DFLs) should reach the beer-check & On-In within five minutes or so of the FRBs. If the slower Hashers say the run was a cake-walk while the FRBs ran their asses off, you've done a great job. On the other hand, too many checks can be quite annoying. In this matter, trail-laying is more of an art than a science. Unfortunately, you can only learn the proper balance from experience, both as Hare and Hound.

Some Inclement Weather Tips:

✳ Rain

✓ Lay your marks larger than normal.

✓ Avoid gutters, where flour is sure to get washed away.

✓ Try to find places to lay trail where the flour won't get wet, if possible.

✓ Flour will stay around better if you lay it in clumps rather than just throwing it on the ground. If you squeeze the clump and set it down it will hold together better.

✓ In rain, flour sticks to wood (trees, fences) better than grass, smooth surfaces or sidewalks.

✓ Be extra careful when laying critical marks (checks, arrows, etc.) because Hounds have a hell of a time figuring out what to do in the absence of trail marks.

✓ Don't bother with chalk, as it *always* gets washed away in the rain.

✓ If rains after you've laid your trail, you really should recheck it before the Hash starts.

✽ Snow (Florida Hashers, disregard!)

✓ Color your flour. Carpenter's snap line powered chalk works well - just be sure to use enough to achieve a distinctly bold color.

✓ Lightly colored flour tends to blend with the snow, making Hash marks difficult - if not impossible - to see.

✓ Hashing in deep snow takes lots of physical effort and your trail should take this fact into account and not be too long.

Starting the Hash

Give a chalk talk before the Hash. This is to acquaint the "new boots" with Hashing in general, and to apprise the old hands of the new twists you've introduced to confound them on the trail.

🦶 Blessing of the Hares

This is an optional prayer offered by the Religious Advisor before the Hash, with local embellishments.

Bless these Hares,
Bless this trail,
Coppus no catch us,
Farmer no shoot us,
Doggus no bite us,
Heatus no stroke us,
Plenty of cold beer to drink us,
Coitus non interruptus.

Now point out the direction of the trail if the pack can't find it themselves in short order.

🦶 Live Hare

✓ Make it clear that you get a fifteen-minute head start.

✓ Enlist a known Auto Hasher as co-conspirator to:

    o Act as the "honest broker" timkeeper.

    o Give the chalk talk (write out the briefing for them).

o   Lead in singing Father Abraham (to assist in providing your full fifteen-minute headstart).

o   Drive the shag vehicle.

o   Facilitate the beer check, if there is one. Just be sure to give your assistant good directions!

The On-In

Probably the most difficult part of Haring is arranging a suitable place for the On-In. This is not an insurmountable problem however, and should not dissuade you from taking your turn as a Hare. Some thoughts follow:

✓ Plan where you want to *end*, and then plan where you want to *start*. There are more starting places than ending places.

✓ Start fairly close (by auto) to the end. The fewer people you have to ferry back to the start, the better. Hares have gotten in trouble this way before.

✓ There should be enough parking space at the start for everyone expected to show up. Also, make sure that it's okay to park there. For some reason Hashers get pissed off when they get back from the On-In and find their cars have been towed! If there isn't sufficient parking space and you simply must use this location, you'll have to gather at another spot where parking is adequate and carpool or shuttle to the start. This adds a degree of complexity to the Hash which isn't recommended under normal circumstances.

✓ While it might seem like a nice idea to have an outdoor On-In, it's by no means guaranteed that the weather will cooperate. Therefore you should plan for an alternate *indoor* On-In site... and watch the weather forecasts!

✓ If ending the Hash at a public establishment (bar, tavern, pub, etc.), coordinate with the owner (or manager) well in advance.

✓ Ask for happy hour prices (or lower, if possible).

✓ Ask about food (free munchies, menu items).

✓ Ask the bar management if pitchers of water and soft drinks can be made available for designated drivers (they may even provide *complimentary* soft drinks).

✓ Get approval for an area of the bar in which to do Hash business. Using a tarp to cover the floor during down-downs is sometimes a wise move.

✓ Point out that the Hash a solemn, serious bunch that is never loud, rambunctious, or lewd (and sell them a bridge in Brooklyn while you are at it...).

Hare responsibilities at the On-In include:

✓ Getting the shag vehicle to the On-In site.

✓ All logistics involved with beer, soft drinks, ice, water, munchies, etc.

✓ Dealing with property owners (both public establishment and private property) in all matters financial and diplomatic.

✓ In public establishments, setting aside sufficient beer for down-downs.

✓ Returning Hashers to the start to retrieve their cars.

✓ Cleaning up the On-In venue after the festivities.

✓ Establishing a Lost & Found for the inevitable misplaced items of personal property.

✓ Hare responsibilities do *not* include the actual conduct of Hash business. This is the sole purview of the Hash Mis-Management.

◗: The On-After and the On-On-On

Just because the On-In is over doesn't mean the fun has to end - especially if your Hash takes place on a Friday or

Saturday. In many Hashes it's common for everyone to move to another venue for an "On-After," and sometimes the truly hardy souls go from there to an "On-On-On." The latter usually takes place at someone's home - often one with a hot tub and/or swimming pool.

Other Hare Responsibilities

In most Hashes the Hares "sweep" trail when Hashers are overdue in order to find DOTs and bring them on-in.

Parting Words

Don't worry about trying to lay the perfect trail - there really is no such thing. Something unforeseen will normally, generally and usually go wrong! Just try your best and your Hash will be a success. Accept your down-down with humility - and don't forget to coordinate with the Beermeister!

Sample Timeline

Get on the hare schedule	Check the Receding Hareline for an open date and notify the Hare Raiser.
Hash minus 30 days	Identify the Hash end location.
Hash minus 30 days	Coordinate with Hash end location owner.
Hash minus 30 days	Begin scouting the trail.
Hash minus 21 days	Identify the Hash start location location.
Hash minus 21 days	Identify the On-Before location.
Hash minus 21 days	Coordinate with On-Before owner.
Hash minus 21 days	Send out eMail publicity info on the Hash.
Hash minus 17 days	Create and reproduce a publicity flyer.
Hash minus 14 days	Distribute the flyer at the preceding Hash.
Hash minus 14 days	Coordinate with the Beermeister.
Hash minus 14 days	Coordinate with helpers (shag wagon, beer check, etc.)
Hash minus 3 days	Final scouting of trail.

Hash minus 3 days	Final coordination with Hash end location owner.
Hash minus 3 days	Final coordination with On-Before location owner.
Hash minus 6 hours	Check weather forecast. Adjust accordingly.
Hash minus 4 hours	Begin laying trail.
Hash minus 90 minutes	Make final logistical preparations.
Hash minus 60 minutes	Go to the On-Before.
Hash minus 30 minutes	Make final coordination with Beermeister, Hash Cash, On-Sec.
Hash minus 15 minutes	Go to the Hash start location.
Hash start	Give chalk talk.

HASH FACT

F.B.A.C. stands for "Fat Boys Athletic Club." It is usually an unofficial and self-claimed subgroup of a kennel.

Religion, also called "the circle," is an important part of Hash tradition and is often the most remembered part of the trail.

Religion, also called "the circle," is an important part of Hash tradition and is often the most remembered part of the trail. With over 1,700 Hashes in the world, there must be at least 1,700 ways to conduct a circle - but the basics are such that most of us would feel right at home in *any* Hash's circle. Religion, after all, is nothing more than a ceremony to mark trail's end, socialize a bit, and award down-downs for achievements... and sins.

A good circle, like anything good, doesn't just *happen*. Conducting one is a lot of work. How do you remember all of the awards and violations you're supposed to hand out? How do you keep the pack's attention? How do you keep people from leaving early or breaking up into private parties? How do you keep things moving and not get bogged down... and how do you know when it's time to quit? A surprising number of tips and techniques come to mind.

There are two philosophies for conducting a circle. One is to try to make everyone happy, and the other is to drive the "posers" away until only the hardcore Hashers are left - who by definition are the ones who *like* the way you run your circle. Most GMs and RAs walk a line between these extremes. They know they can't make everybody happy, but at the same time don't want their Hash to shrink and turn cretinous through inbreeding.

If your Hash has a good solid membership and long-standing circle traditions, don't mess with them. When Hashers are happy, it's best to leave things be! If you've been conducting good circles with a high level of attention and participation from the pack, don't change a thing - but having said that, if your circle is disorganized and you find yourself shouting to be heard over the sound of private parties and slamming car doors as Hashers leave early, you might want to consider some of the following suggestions:

🦶 Disorganize Yourself

Write out a list of the main down-downs and awards you plan to present. Use a small piece of paper, or just write on the back of your hand. A typical list contains Hares, virgins, visitors, naming, Hashit award, violations, whistle check, etc.

🦶 Plan a Schedule

Allow some time for Hashers to come on-in and catch their breath. Allocate thirty to forty-five minutes for the circle. Also have a plan for On-Afters, and for moving the pack on to On-Afters after the circle is over.

🦶 Learn More than One Down-Down Song

The pack can get pretty bored singing "He's true blue" over and over. See the mini-hymnal in this book for some tried and true selections, or download the full Hash songbook and learn some new ones.

🦶 Have the Funniest, Loudest Hasher Lead Circle

This works for some Hashes. "Chuck E. Cheeks" of the Denver HHH can keep people in stitches for hours, and so can "Reverend Itchy" of the San Francisco H3 - but the downside is your "perfect RA" won't always be there, and when you have to stand in you're going to look and sound like Ben Stein by comparison. "Bueller….. Bueller….."

🦶 Expose Yourself

This'll get everyone's attention the first couple of times you try it, or if you are female, the first dozen times, but after a while… well, you'll soon agree with the late "Zippy" (may he Hash in peace!) who once said he'd seen so many naked Hashers that his *new* sexual fantasy was mentally *dressing* them. Besides, some Hashers have problems with nudity - and you'll risk losing them.

🦶 Punish Private Parties

To me this depends on how long down-downs have been going on. If people are having private parties right from the start, call 'em up for down-downs and set an example. The pack owes the circle a certain amount of respect, after all! But if the circle has been dragging on for more than an hour, remember that it's only natural for people to want to visit with their friends - and maybe private parties are a hint your circle has been going on too long.

🦶 Give the Pack Time to Socialize

As the pack comes in, let them drink, snack and socialize for ten to twenty minutes before starting the circle. This will get most of the visiting out of the way. Conversely, don't wait too long to start the circle, or people will begin to drift off.

👣 Limit Terroristic Down-Downs

Unless your Hash routinely makes everyone sit bare-assed on the ice or kneel while Hashers pour flour and ice water over their heads (and everyone in your Hash is used to it), try to limit the really harsh down-downs to the hardcore members of your circle. Many potential Hashers have been frightened away by down-downs like these. Then again, if your definition of "potential Hasher" is someone who won't be frightened away, harsh on, dude!

👣 Avoid Individuals Doing Multiple Down-Downs

The Hash world, while honest and forthcoming in all other matters, doesn't like to talk about the Hashers who've been caught driving home drunk, so numbers are hard to come by. It probably happens way more often than most of us realize, so take that into account when doling out down-downs.

👣 Avoid Numerous Namings

Try not to forget that namings seem to take even longer for the Hashers getting named, and to the new or visiting Hashers who are excluded from the naming circle.

👣 Limit Volatile Violations

Opening the floor for violation nominations from the pack, especially if they're pretty drunk already, is a mistake. "Guerilla down-downs" quickly deteriorate into silliness and sometimes harassment of individuals: "I nominate Creamsicle because she has a nose!" Sure, you can ask pack members if they observed violations of Hash etiquette, but violation nominations should come from you, and you should limit them to two or three.

Abundant Awards

Most Hashes award a Hashit, but some kennels give additional awards. One Hash which comes to mind is an extreme example, with awards including the Hashit, the FRB Award, the Best Dressed Award, the Stud of Sadism, the Prestigious Bitch, the Menacing Manacles of Masochism, and some I probably don't even know about yet.

Pack Pimping

If you don't have a plan, or if you have one but don't stick to it, pretty soon the pack will take over, shouting out things like, "You forgot the Hares, new shoes, whistle check, birthdays, etc." At that point you might as well join the pack!

Dickhead Debates

Establish clear policies prior to the circle, otherwise you'll wind up arguing with members of the pack over whether visiting Hashers have to do Virgin Hasher down-downs, or whether Virgins have to do repeat down-downs because they don't have whistles.

72

Have a Plan for Concluding the Circle

Think about how and when you're going to conclude formalities and get the pack moving to the On-After. Try to keep the circle to forty-five minutes maximum, and always end it with the singing of the International Hash Hymn (*Swing Low, Sweet Chariot*), followed by a formal announcement that the circle is over. This way the pack knows what you're doing and what's coming next, and they're less likely to interrupt you with things you missed - and you'll always miss *something!*

HASH FACT
The 'Deep Freeze' Hash House Harriers and 'Brass Monkey' Hash House Harriers run in Antarctica.

TERMS

"HOUND"

Like many other sub-cultures, Hashing has a language of its own...

"Are You?" (RU?)	Question shouted by the pack to FRBs, meaning "Are you on the trail?"
Back Check	Trail mark indicating that back tracking is necessary in order to find the true trail because the true trail branches off prior to the check mark.
Back Hare Sweep Hare Sweeper Checking Chicken	Hare who remains with the last runners to make sure everyone makes it on-in.
Bash	Bicycle Hash.
Beer Check	Beverage stop or trail mark indicating a beverage stop.
Beermeister	The person who supplies the beer, soda, water, and chips for the Hash.
Check	Trail mark indicating the true trail must be sorted out from the false trails.

Circle	Assembly of Hashers at trail's end, normally for the purpose of conducting down-downs.
"Checking"	Answer shouted by FRBs to pack when asked "Are You?" indicating he has not determined whether the trail he's following is true or false.
Down-Down	The ceremony of quaffing a beverage in one go (an honor!)
False Trail/YBF (You've Been F*ked)	A short trail which ends with a Tee sign, three lines, or other mark indicating termination.
FRB	Front-Running Bastard: Faster members of the pack, or the first to arrive at the on-in.
Grand Master/Mistress (GM)	Mismanagement member, ceremonial leader of the Hash. This term is, in many Hashes, given to the Hash Master/Mistress after his/her tenure.
Grand Mattress (GM)	Synonym for Grand Mistress.

Haberdasher	Mismanagement member in charge of T-shirts, hats, mementos, etc.
Hare	Hasher who lays the trail.
Hare Raiser	Mismanagement member in charge of lining up Hares for future trails.
Harrierette	Female Hasher.
Hash Cash	Mismanagement member; Hash equivalent of Treasurer.
Hash Flash	Designated photographer for Hash events.
Hash Horn	Mismanagement member; Carries a horn or bugle on trail and blows it to encourage and guide the pack.
Hash House	The Selangor Club in Kuala Lumpur, meeting place of the Mother Hash.
Hash House Harrier/Harriette	Any Hasher.
Hash Name	Nickname, usually bestowed after a set number of runs, or in honor of a notable incident.

Hash Trash	Newsletter, usually with reports of previous Hashes and a list of upcoming events.
Hash Shit	Offensive or embarrassing object awarded to a Hasher for notable on-trail accomplishments. Normally carried by the awardee on subsequent trails until it is "earned" by someone else.
Hashing	The act of running a Hash trail.
Held/Hold Check	Trail mark indicating an intersection where true trail may take another direction, but requires Hashers to wait until ordered by the Hare to "check it out."
Horrors	Children of Hashers.
Hounds	The body of Hashers in pursuit of the Hare; they comprise the Pack.
Interhash	International Hash gathering.
Kennel or Chapter	Local Hash group.

Live Hare	Hare who gets a nominal head start and is pursued by the pack as he or she lays trail.
Mismanagement	Hash officials; Sometimes elected, sometimes appointed, always drunk.
Nash Nash	A *national* gathering of Hashers.
"On Call"	Shouted in response to "Are you?" by Hashers to indicate that while they do not see any trail markings, they are following someone else's "On On" calls.
On-In or On-Inn	Trail's end, or trail mark indicating the end is near.
"On On"	Shouted by FRBs or any Hounds to indicate they are on true trail. Only shouted by a Hasher to indicate they see *true trail* markings. See also "On Call."
On Sec	Mismanagement member normally in charge of Hash rosters, run records, etc.

Puppies	Children of Hashers; see "Horrors."
Receding Hareline	List of up-and-coming Hash events, normally printed in the Hash Trash.
Religious Advisor (RA)	Mismanagement member, often in charge of Circle, also in charge of blessing the Hash and settling disputes over tradition. Also responsible for the weather!
Scribe	Mismanagement member normally in charge of writing "The Words."
SCB	Short-Cutting Bastard; habitual short-cutter.
Shiggy	Thick vegetation, streams, etc; especially mud. Some Hashes believe if you're not in shiggy, you're not Hashing!
Sweeper	see "Back Hare."
Virgin	Hash newbie; first-time Hasher.

HASH FACT

Founder Albert Stephen Ignatius Gispert was known as 'G' to his friends but was actually born Alberto Esteban Ignacio Gispert in Greenwich, London, and was the son of Catalonian immigrants.

HASH MARKS

While many trail marks are "standard," it's important to attend the Chalk Talk to learn which are used by a particular Hash.

●.....................TRAIL

A blob of flour indicates a trail. Three consecutive Hash marks indicates *true* trail.

⊗..............CHECK

Indicates that the trail may change direction at this point. Here Hounds spread out and look for trail. From the check, true trail will begin again in about 100 yards in any direction.

☰..........FALSE TRAIL

Three parallel lines across the trail indicate that the trail is false and the Hounds should return to the last check to look for the true trail.

↑.....................TRUE TRAIL

Laid only by Hares. A Hare arrow always indicates true trail. Hounds may also mark arrows, but Hound arrows lack the three Hash marks on the shaft and may or may not indicate true trail.

BN ....BEER NEAR

Indicates there's beer within 100 yards or so. When used to indicate a beer check, Front Running Bastards (FRBs) must wait until the Dead Fu*king Last (DFL) Hounds arrives before proceeding on trail.

® ....REGROUP

Indicates that the Hounds must wait and regroup the pack at this point. FRBs must wait until the DFL Hound arrives before proceeding on trail. Sometimes uses an "H" and called a "Hash Halt."

T Y E TURKEY/EAGLE SPLIT

At this point the trail splits into a segment which is easy (turkey) and a segment which is difficult (eagle).

W ....BOOB CHECK

This is a check wherein only females may look for trail - and the pack cannot proceed until a woman finds it. Sometimes a circle with a dot in the center. Good Harrierettes flash the pack when they see this symbol!

Other "nonstandard" marks are also used at the discretion of the Hares. These include, but are not limited to: back checks, dick checks, photo op, etc. When nonstandard marks are used they must be fully explained during the chalk talk!

Beer Soup For the Hasher's Soles

HASH NAMES

"Let's call her 'Tastes Like Chicken'!"

> **Just like the name your parents gave you, you don't get to pick your Hash name!**

If you are a Virgin Hasher you may be wondering what sort of name you might get, and if you are a veteran you may be thinking how to best name some deserving wanker. Keep in mind there's a story behind most of them. A Hasher named "DQ," for example, is fast enough to have won a variety of 10K races, but his Hash name has nothing to do with speed. Instead it comes from the day he stopped mid-Hash at a Dairy Queen for a snack.

"Stroke Her" spends her non-Hashing spare time involved in rowing competitions. "Clueless" is, well, you'd have to know him to appreciate how appropriate the name is. "Red Square" started Hashing in Moscow. "Semper Bi" is a former female Marine who *once* did the wild thing with another woman. "Sheila" is actually a *he* who made the mistake of running with a bunch of Australian Hashers who had a hard time pronouncing his last name - and so he became "Sheila," Aussie slang for a woman.

As you might expect, a common Hash name is "Blowjob." You need only be seen blowing up a balloon, putting air into your car tire, or giving the GM oral sex to be bestowed that title for the rest of your Hashing days.

"Cunning Linguist" is another extremely common Hash name, and comes from a sexual act - but of course you knew that. It is usually given to multi-lingual Hashers... although some have earned it the old fashioned way!

Then there's "Eager Beaver," "Ben Dover" and "All Hands On Dick," which are more or less self explanatory, and two of my favorites - "A-Lick-A-Ho" (a Native American lesbian) and her girlfriend, "Finger In the Dyke."

Just like the name your parents gave you, you don't get to pick your Hash name. It's awarded to you in a christening ceremony based on some notable accomplishment, weird physical characteristic, or for no reason at all other than a collective whim. Naming ceremonies take strange twists.

Take "Road Kill," for example, a veteran Hasher who had started out as "Crazy Annie." She got renamed during one very dark and stormy night of Hashing when she kept wandering into the street in front of oncoming traffic because her glasses were fogged over.

What if you don't like your Hash name? Well, complain about it enough and you're sure to be rechristened - with something much, much worse! For example, "Shithead" of the Capital H3 wanted to be renamed... so they changed his name to "Fucking Shithead." He didn't learn his lesson and asked to be renamed *again*, so now they call him "Stupid Fucking Shithead." He finally shut up!

HASH FACT

The Hash Handle given to John Wayne Bobbitt, who runs in the Las Vegas Hash, is "A Stitch in Time Saved Mine"...

Beer Soup For the Hasher's Soles

HASH TALES

Not surprisingly, some pretty funny things happen when a bunch of drunken wankers follow a flour trail in search of beer... and who doesn't like to see their name in print?

WORLD'S BIGGEST LAUGH
Police expose world's biggest hash ring!

A police internet expert was sure that he was on the track of the world's biggest hash ring, with more than 160,000 members in a worldwide organization. And he found out that there was a Danish man behind it, living in Aarhus.

Red-faced police in Aarhus had to admit to *Ekxtra Bladet* yesterday that they had found instead an organization of thirsty cross-country runners with the name Hash House Harriers.

Just the word "hash" got the policeman excited. He found out, after a quick look on the internet, that the Hash House Harriers are to organize a big hash-event in Denmark next year (Interhash 99). He pictured 160,000 hash wrecks in the country of the little mermaid. So he alerted his colleagues.

The policeman from Nordjyland didn't think to keep on reading the screen, nor does he understand too much English. He convinced the drug police in Aarhus that a big case was ready to be solved. Even the telephone number of the hash contact person was given on the internet.

The busy policeman with the limited reading skills did not realize that the Hash House Harriers are the world's biggest club for cross-country runners. At Aarhus police station this hint from a colleague in another district was taken seriously.

"I was shocked when I was called in for questioning,

where the accusation was that I had something to do with hash," said thirty-two-year-old Tommy Roenn (aka "Charlie Brown") of Aarhus, the contact person for the Aarhus Hash House Harriers. He runs the EDP consulting company Alpha Tech at Jaegergardsgade.

"Afterwards I could see that it was a funny story, but that was not what I was thinking of in the situation when I was called for a third degree questioning!"

"I was told that the police had tried several times to get hold of me at my address. On Wednesday, a summons from the police said that I had to show up for a meeting on Thursday at 10 AM. I called them and asked what it was all about, and was told it had something to do with drug smuggling. They had found my name on the internet."

After they threatened to pick him up physically, Roenn offered to show up at the police station immediately - and he took all kinds of material about the Hash House Harriers with him.

"I reckon they still thought that it was a drug issue, even though I told them everything about our running club. However, they accepted all the material. Among other things, there was a video of a run which showed what we are doing."

Roenn was recently in Malaysia to celebrate the club's 60th anniversary, and as he had also been on runs in Belgium, Holland and Germany at various times it is easy to see what the police pictured for themselves. He was the perfect hash courier!

"'Hash House' means cheap food and service. After

accusing me, the police did not look on the internet to check out further pages where everything was explained."

Roenn explained that the Hash House Harriers were founded by British soldiers in 1938, more or less by chance. They were bored in Kuala Lumpur and figured out that a run was better than having another 'hair of the dog' the morning after. Since then the organization has grown to 160,000 members.

"It was all about celebrating after a good run with a beer or two. And the rules are still the same."

"Do you smoke hash?"

"NEVER. Our only drug is beer, and in fact our main sponsor is Carlsberg. The club has sixty members in Aarhus and three hundred in Copenhagen, and in fact many of them are policemen..."

Translated from the Danish newspaper *Ekxtra Bladet* where it appeared on November 27, 1998.

HASH FACT

The idea of a nighttime run under the rays of a full moon is of uncertain origin, but San Diego formed a Full Moon kennel in 1986 - and this was possibly was the first. While often claiming independence, Full Moon Hashes are usually closely linked to a 'mainstream' Hash.

CROSS EXAMINING
A Cross Dresser

Major William Scott Bradley and I followed very similar paths in life, at least from a geographical standpoint. I first met him in New York when he was an enlisted man in the Marine reserve, and later on he was my platoon commander in Okinawa as a First Lieutenant. But that wasn't the end of our encounters. Not by a long shot.

He and I crossed paths once again at Camp Pendleton late in my career. The Major and I worked together on a couple of field exercises, but most of our contact came through a running club to which we both belonged. More about that later.

One fine day I received a call asking me to appear as a character witness on Major Bradley's behalf. A Woman Marine in his command had charged him with sexual harassment. It was the holiday season, and a few of the females in the unit had dressed in skimpy "elf" costumes to liven up the Company Christmas party. The Major's offense consisted of making the statement, "Those sure are some sexy elves!" or words to that effect. That's all.

I ended up testifying at the Major's court martial hearing because I, like the Major, was a member of the local Hash House Harrier chapter. I must explain that the HHH is billed as an "international drinking club with a running problem."

The club itself is a harmless diversion, although on *that* day the prosecutor made it sound like something akin to the indulgences of Caligula!

At one point in my testimony I was asked if I knew the Major's "Hash Name." Those names are usually risqué, often take the form of a double entendre, and are bestowed upon a Hasher as part of his or her initiation. Some of them are actually quite funny. I answered in the affirmative, but didn't want to volunteer the name unless I was directed to. I was.

"Yes, Sir, the Major's name is Cross Dresser," I told them. As you can imagine there was quite a bit of snickering in the courtroom, and even the presiding officer was laughing out loud. I guess they don't hear that sort of testimony every day.

That name, along with the statement he allegedly made, was the entire case. Maybe it's just me, but there must have been *something* more constructive the dozen or so Marines in that courtroom could have been doing that day.

I'm just glad they didn't ask me what *my* name was.

This is an edited version of a story which originally appeared in the book *Swift, Silent and Surrounded.*

HASH FACT

A Photo Hash is a Hash where the pack is given photographs of the next check (i.e. some famous or recognizable local landmark) and have to thus navigate themselves around. Can be fun, but it's not really Hashing, so it shouldn't be done too often.

DOWN-DOWN SHOWDOWN
In Margaritaville

On winter afternoons in Old Colorado City, a pleasant suburb of Colorado Springs, residents do not expect sixty or more men and women to mass in tiny Bott Park, all dressed in summer garb - Hawaiian shirts, shorts, sarongs, and Panama hats.

But one Saturday last February, they did.

Nor do they expect to hear a hunter's horn blow, as if calling hounds to a fox. And they certainly do not expect to then witness a wildly dressed mob sprint off toward the countryside of Bear Creek and beyond.

But one Saturday last February, they did.

To innocent observers in that residential neighborhood, with all the undulating color - pinks, tangerines, violets - it must have seemed as if some tropical cruise ship had popped its seams. A few of the runners even lugged cross-country skis - and most snow in the area had melted days before.

If a concerned citizen had summoned police, the explanation would have been equally loony. It was the start of the Margaritaville Run, hosted by the Pikes Peak Hash House Harriers. Even more weird, the Hashers (a running club) had invited the Colorado Parrot Heads (a Jimmy Buffett fan club) to join them for the first time in a kind of party-warrior test of mettle.

It was the most simpatico of mergers, or so insisted an individual who was a proud honorary member of both groups. This same person lured the emphatically non-burly Parrot Heads to participate by telling deliberate, outlandish lies. Among them:

❖ Parrot Heads were reassured that the run-ski trail was actually a pleasant walking course selected to generate thirst without generating sweat.

❖ Hashers were promised that Parrot Heads were feisty outdoor vets but also easy drunks who, after only a couple margaritas, were generous with free tickets to Buffett concerts.

❖ Downhill skis, he went on, were just as serviceable as cross-country equipment because skiing wasn't required.

Lies, damn lies, all lies. What species of treacherous, low-life, double-crossing fiend would resort to such tactics? Me, the treacherous lying fiend.

I had cause. Parrot Heads and Hash House Harriers (H3s) rank among the world's most eccentric social organizations, and Colorado's enclaves of each are shining, oddball examples. If these groups met in a one-day revolt against snow, slush, and many things Gore-Tex there might be chemistry, there might even be alchemy - but something interesting would surely result.

Beer Soup For the Hasher's Soles

The Parrot Heads and Hashers had introductory drinks at Beau Jo's Bar in Old Colorado City as a prelude to embarking on a customized Margaritaville-style run-plus-ski (beverage stops included). I watched with a puppeteer's appreciation as Hashers and Heads mingled in the crowded bar. Nearly everyone was sporting tropical garb, yet differences were apparent. Although H3 members call themselves a "drinking club with a running problem," they at least wore appropriate shoes - low hikers or trail running shoes. The Parrot Heads, on the other hand, were dressed unambiguously as non-athletes. I leaned in to listen as ultra-marathoner Michelle Stoll approached a female Parrot Head who was lounging comfortably at the bar. Stoll considered the woman's boots and blue jeans for a moment before she asked, "Do you really think you're going to be able to run a rough trail dressed like that?"

The woman smiled at Michelle's sleek running tights, sucked on her cigarette for effect, then replied, amused, as she exhaled, "I've got pockets. At least I won't have to go around begging someone to carry my smokes and lighter."

There were more sparks later when a Hasher suggested to Ruthie Guthrey, a spiritual Parrot Head since 1974, that she tell fellow members to pack a few beers in the event they wanted to rehydrate while on the trail.

"You don't need to tell us about partying!" Guthrey bristled. As evidence, she described the battery-powered blender that club members carry on field trips and in other wilderness situations. "We know how to handle ourselves under survival conditions," she added. "Try standing in the rain three or four hours, waiting for Jimmy to sing. We're professionals."

Yes, the tension was palpable, and egos were on exhibit. It was high noon in Old Colorado City. There were fins to the left, fins to the right. A lot of pride was on the line.

When it comes to partying, no group enjoys more nationwide cachet than the Parrot Heads. Established in Atlanta in 1989, and known officially as Parrot Heads in Paradise (PHP), Buffett's disciples have utilized the man's music as scaffolding for a passionate lifestyle that celebrates all that's affirmative and tropical.

"It's not just an organization," Todd Rule told me. "Being a Parrot Head is a way of living. A very positive, fun way of life." Rule, along with his wife, Maureen, founded the Colorado club in '94 - and said that they and a portion of their 250-plus members participate in Parrot Head events almost every week. Oddly, ski weekends are no longer scheduled. Rule told me they tried one a long time back, but not a single Parrot Head showed up.

Unbelievable. There are more than 170 PHP clubs around the world, and many of them do group ski trips - but not the Denver-based group. "We don't claim to be a club for athletes," he said.

Like the parent organization, the Colorado Parrot Heads also take the charity work they do seriously. "We'll hold these great events, have a blast, and give all the proceeds to good causes," Rule says. "It's what we love to do."

Standing in Beau Jo's, Rule seemed less enthusiastic about the run. He and the other Parrot Heads had arrived at the bar an hour earlier than everyone else, and they'd found their margarita rhythm, so they were reluctant to abandon cold drinks and warm seats for the outdoors.

"Something that worries me," Rule said, "is the Hashers say even they don't know how long the course is. They say they *never* know in advance."

True. "Hares" lay a trail of chalk or flour in secret, complete with several false trails and at least one beverage stop.

"An easy walk," I told him. "Don't worry."

Rule replied, "Good. It's like Jimmy would say: 'Some people treat their bodies like a temple. We treat ours like tents.'"

While the Parrot Heads seem to have elevated partying to art, few organizations rival the Hash House Harriers when it comes to promoting innovative, bizarre party skills.

According to the World Hash Handbook, the organization was started in 1938 at the Selangor Club in Kuala Lumpur, Malaysia where the British expatriates' mess was known as the Hash House. Members held a hare-and-hounds run that ended with much drinking and singing. The event was such a success, they gave it a name and kept running. Today, there are clubs in more than 130 countries with many thousands of members. Pikes Peak H3 of Colorado Springs, and its sister club, the PMS Women's Hash (they run every 28 days!) are among the most active.

Bruce "Slugbust" Huber, a longtime member, told me, "I love the traditions. It's considered impolite to be competitive on the trail. People who finish at the front - the Front

Running Bastards, or FRBs - are singled out for punishment: what we call a 'down-down.'" To be sentenced to a down-down is to be made to chug a beverage (you don't have to drink alcohol to belong anymore). "The run is still just an excuse to have a party afterward," says Slugbust. "That part of Hashing will never change."

When the 2 PM starter's horn sounded at precisely 2:32 PM, more than five dozen runners dressed like Buffett clones jogged off through winter streets following blue chalk marks. The first part of the trail took us through an area of rugged brush, up a hillside, then across a creek. There'd been snow all week until the previous day - when a heat wave melted it. Now it was cold again, but muddy - unpleasant conditions for running, or walking, or skiing.

At first, I hung back with the Parrot Heads. After two miles or so of arduous slogging though, I decided to put some distance between us when I perceived a growing animus directed at me. This was reconfirmed every time I topped a ridge on that evil path. When Parrot Heads spotted me from below, they'd shout, "We're going to have your Florida-loving butt for this, Rando! You'll regret the day you did this to us!"

They were right. I did regret it - and much sooner than they'd hoped. An hour into the route, I saw what I thought were Hashers on a far hillside. Believing I was taking a shortcut (not allowed), I bushwacked for another half hour only to discover that the Hashers were actually strollers from a nearby gated community.

I was so lost that I had to telephone for directions - a taboo guaranteed to earn several down-downs at the after-run awards ceremony known as the Hash Circle. ("It's kind of like a Kangaroo Court where people are sometimes honored, sometimes humiliated, but mostly always both," explained Terry "Rat's Ass" Weathers, one of the founders of Pikes Peak H3).

I was filthy and exhausted by the time I made my way to the short ski section. I had the option of first resting at the rehydration stop (beer and piña coladas). The weak and the wise did exactly that. Not me. Face your fears - that's my motto. Years ago, during my only alpine skiing experience, I wore skis into the lodge's restroom and was traumatized by the distance that separated me from the urinal. I was eager to put this second skiing nightmare astern.

I didn't. Wearing cross-country skis, I slogged through stretches of orange mud that were interrupted by micro-seconds of sheer terror on patches of sheet ice. We'd walk, slog, then ski a little. Then we'd walk and slog some more, only to hit a long lane of ice, and suddenly we'd be rocketing down the hillside on a collision course with the next long stretch of mud and rock.

A couple of Parrot Heads had come along to watch. They slurped their beverages and held cigarettes at jaunty angles while offering downhill tips. On one particularly ugly trail - a hillside of rotten snow and iron oxide - they endeared themselves by muling gear without complaint.

Good people, those Parrot Heads.

It was here, on an icy grade, that ultra-marathoner Stoll took a very nasty spill - and then tried to blame me just because I'd used her as an emergency braking device. Absurd!

Finally, though, I limped into the beer stop at Rat's Ass's plush home. There I found Parrot Heads and Hashers swilling margaritas like old pals, trying to steel themselves before they attempted the ski section, all laughing at my distress. Michele Gandy empathized. She'd arrived only slightly before me. "That was like the Trail of Tears, man. I needed oxygen. If someone kidnaps me and makes me do another Hash, I'll never leave the bar."

Veteran Hasher Tony "No Girth" Sharer, who was using a blender powered by a weed-whacker gas engine to make daiquiris, paid her a compliment - and Hashers aren't known for flattery. "I give you guys credit, you didn't quit. I don't think we'll see you on the trail again. Hell, we'd of had to been running backward to see you *this* time. But the partying part, at least, you clearly know your stuff."

Then, as No Girth held up a fresh pitcher, he tipped his tropical straw hat. Attached to the top was a stuffed, life-sized artificial parrot.

HASH FACT

On April Fool's Day, 2006, Atlanta H3 announced that they would thereafter be known as *Happy* House Harries as "the Hash part of the name attracted the wrong kind of clientele - hippies and drug users - and at the same time put off the right kind - beer-swilling, jogging-happy party-animals."

NO HATE INTENDED

Police Examine Possible Hate Crime

The following two stories were printed in the Dallas Morning News on consecutive days, with the first appearing on Sunday, February 21, 1993:

Two groups of young white men with shaved heads ran through an Old East Dallas apartment complex Saturday spreading a white powder in what police are investigating as a possible hare crime.

The men threw the powder on the ground and playground equipment at the Roseland Homes apartments in the 2100 block of North Washington before fleeing, police said.

One of the men gave two children necklaces of colored beads, and another man carried what appeared to be a small, shrunken head, Officer Larry Dyer said. Witnesses told police that some of the men chanted unintelligibly and did not respond to residents' questions.

Police have sent samples of the powder to a lab for testing and expect results in three weeks. Even if the powder is not harmful, the incident could be filed as a hate crime, Detective Sandra Ortega DeKing said.

"Either way, it probably would be a hate crime because white males did this in Roseland Homes, which is predominantly black," she said.

Apartment resident Aretha Franklin said the powder was

disturbing. "I want to know what the substance was because kids play in the playground," she said.

Four of the men ran through the apartment playground Saturday morning and returned in the afternoon with four to six other men, police said. They carried the powder in plastic-covered bags.

During the incident at about 2:30 PM, witnesses told police, the men began spreading the powder at the J.W. Ray Elementary School playground across the street. One man made an "X" on the ground with the white powder.

They were last seen getting into a yellow van with the word "Remco" written on the side, police were told.

The follow-up story from Monday, February 22:

Delbert Hirst of Arlington 'fessed up Sunday. He was one of the white males seen spreading "white powder" Saturday throughout a predominantly black apartment complex in Old East Dallas.

He doesn't see anything wrong with it. In fact he does things like that most weekends in similar areas of Fort Worth. He sees it as harmless fun.

Some people in Dallas, including police, were baffled by the mysterious action. The Police Department began an investigation the incident as a possible hate crime.

"I was shocked so much was being made out of it," Mr. Hirst said Sunday. "I guess it just shows how sensitive things must really be over there when it comes to racial issues."

Mr. Hirst is part of an international "social" running group called the Hash House Harriers. The Dallas-Fort Worth chapter meets Saturdays, often to enjoy a human version of "the hare and the hound."

Police said Saturday that they were investigating the powder spreading as a hate crime "because the white males did this in Roseland Homes, which is predominantly black."

Police also sent out samples of the powder for testing. If Mr. Hirst is correct, the lab will find it is a substance common to kitchens and supermarkets: flour. The runners use it to make their trail.

The runners' fun turned serious Saturday, when residents of the apartments at 2100 North Washington Avenue told police that they thought Mr. Hirst and two other men were committing a hate crime.

Residents described the men as "skinheads" because of "the way they dress and because their heads were shaved," according to a police offense report.

The men put the powder in the grass, around the base of a tree, inside a tire where children play and in a tunnel area, residents told police. The men also handed beads to children and spread more powder on a nearby playground.

Residents told police that they believed the men were skinheads trying to poison children.

If that behavior wasn't strange enough, the men "ran through the complex chanting as though they were worshipping some type of god," the report read. One man even carried a shrunken head, residents told police.

The Hash House Harriers act that way on purpose to blow

off stress, Mr. Hirst said. They sometimes dress in outlandish costumes and run through neighborhoods, wooded areas and other parts of town to spice up their daily running routine.

"We can run on the street anytime," he said.

Mr. Hirst was one of three "Hares" who scoped out a trail for the "Hounds" to follow Saturday.

The Hares were leading the group of twenty-one runners to the Mardi Gras parade on McKinney Avenue.

To mark a trail for the Hounds to follow, the Hares use flour to mark X's and other signs so that runners know they are on the trail. As for the skinhead look, the Hares had military-style haircuts because it turns out they are National Guard members. The third man is balding naturally.

The chanting that was reposted was from runners yelling, "On! On!" to let stray runners know they were on the trail and "Check!" when they reached a mark on the trail distinguishing a checkpoint.

The shrunken head, it turns out, was a mannequin's head that one runner carries as a token. All members in the group have nicknames. The head-bearing runner, of course, is "Deadhead."

"We like to go to places we don't normally go," said Mr. Hirst, an Arlington landscape architect, "People usually avoid places and are afraid of areas where a lot of black people live. We weren't."

He said the group has run through the Como neighborhood in Fort Worth, a predominantly black section of town, as well as similar areas in east Fort Worth.

"And they love it," he said. "They laugh and think it's a

parade because we're all dressed up."

As the Hash House group ran through Roseland Homes on Saturday, some runners handed children Mardi Gras beads as a gesture of friendship, Hirst added.

"I was incredulous that an innocent group like ours would get that kind of reaction," Hash House member Robin Doglio said. "It really underscores the racial tensions in Dallas."

Detective Stan Southall said the explanation sounds plausible, but the Department's Intelligence Unit will continue to investigate to make sure Mr. Hirst's story checks out.

"I'm not surprised of the conclusion jumped to by everybody, given the recent past history of events," he said, "but the story did make my day."

HASH FACT

Shandy is a mixture of beer and a soft drink, traditionally ginger ale, although these days it is more likely to be lemonade. It has a bit of a 'girlie' or 'poofter' stigma to it, but is in fact an ideal drink when really thirsty, i.e. at the end of a run. Mother Hashers were quite keen on it, making it the *original* Hash drink!

POWDER MYSTERY SOLVED

William Hermann and Christina Leonard

Phoenix police and firefighters will remember it as "The Mystery of the White Powder."

The call came about 10:30 AM on Monday. A citizen alerted the Phoenix Fire Department that Daisy, his golden retriever, became ill after eating white powder off a sidewalk in the Moon Valley area, near Ninth Avenue and Thunderbird Road.

"The man told us his dog sniffed and licked the stuff and came back in the house and vomited," Division Chief Terry Garrison said. "The guy put two and two together and figured there might be something very wrong with that white powder."

The firefighters hit the street. Those first at the scene found a daunting sight - white powder all through the neighborhood.

It was deposited in odd, arrowlike stripes on the sidewalks, and a breeze had apparently scattered it onto lawns and landscaping stones.

"Our people said, 'Hey, this could be hazardous material. We better take some precautions,'" Garrison said.

The fire department sent twelve big fire engines to the scene, carrying a total of about sixty firefighters.

The Phoenix Police Department sent eight motorcycle officers, one motorcycle sergeant, one motorcycle lieutenant, two field officers, one field sergeant, one detective and a public information officer, a spokesman said.

The cops closed off an area of about two square miles. Children at the local elementary and middle schools were kept inside. Neighbors were warned not to get near the mysterious white stuff.

Some firefighters gathered samples of the powder. Most sat for hours under the shade of trees and fire truck umbrellas, with their navy blue T-shirts soaked with sweat from the 106-degree heat.

Some chatted with nearby golfers.

Some complained.

Many cheered when the fire department's "goody" truck showed up, stocked with fresh Gatorade and trail mix.

One local resident emerged from his house, gazed around in wonder, and asked police who had been murdered.

Television news reporters reported the white powder crisis as their 5 PM lead story on at least two stations, and it led the 10 PM news on most stations.

The fire department called in a hazardous-material company to vacuum up the substance. Children were removed from harm's way and driven home on buses or by worried parents.

Finally, at 11 PM, the six men operating the huge vacuum cleaners were finished. The firefighters and the cops packed up and departed. Residents went to bed.

And as they slept, an anonymous caller to the fire department solved the mystery of the white powder. Garrison said it was a woman who declined to leave her name.

"She said she was with a jogging club, and they had put flour on the sidewalks Saturday to mark where people were supposed to jog in an event they had," Garrison said. "She said she was real sorry, and hung up."

This story originally appeared in *The Arizona Republic* on September 10, 1997.

HASH FACT

Of all the various Hashshit trophies that have been used, it is the toilet seat that is the most common. Nepal H3 claims this dates to Prince Charles' Royal Visit to Nepal, when a specially constructed toilet was made for his Royal Highness and afterwards destroyed so that nobody else could have claimed to have 'sat on the royal throne.'

RED HERRINGS
In Red Dresses

Darrell Laurant

Even as long as I've been in this business, I still encounter something new nearly every week. Until last Sunday afternoon, for instance, I'd never interviewed a man who was wearing a hoop skirt and running shoes.

"Running in this won't be easy," said Frank McPhatter as he stood in the parking lot behind Frametome. "But it looks good, don't you think?"

McPhatter was competing in the annual Valentine's Day Red Dress Run sponsored by the Seven Hills Hash House Harriers, and he had borrowed the hoop from his wife's wedding dress to do it. All around him were others who had made their own compromises between fashion and ease of movement.

We ran a photo of this event on our front page last year and received a few phone calls from people who misinterpreted the purpose (or lack of purpose) of the Red Dress Run. If I get any calls after this column, I'm going to refer them all to Richard Morrison, one of the "Hares" for this year's event. Morrison used to be a defensive lineman for Notre Dame. One Sunday he was wearing a long blonde wig that made him look like a cross between Darryl Hannah and Rick Flair. Or I could refer them to Ed Howell, a Marine stationed at Quantico who met his wife at a Hash and then *married* her at a Hash.

"We were the Hares, and the other people in the wedding reception had to chase us," said his wife Lynda, who looked a lot better in her red dress than Ed.

According to Paul Stark, a.k.a. "Pink Panther," Hashing originated among some Brits stationed in Malaysia during the colonial era.

"This one guy used to go out and run off his hangovers every morning," Panther said. "Some of his friends were laughing at him, and he said, 'I'll bet you can't catch me." So he laid out this trail."

From those humble, hangover beginnings have emerged more than 1,200 Hash groups in 150 countries. But there's more to it than just following a four or five mile spoor. Experienced Hares learn to lay down false trails that tend to penalize the faster runners.

"What usually happens," Morrison said, "is that everybody winds up at the finish line about the same time." Except for those that get lost.

"Usually, that's the people who try to take a short cut," Lynda Howell said.

I asked her what her "Hash name" was and she told me. "I can't put that in the newspaper," I said. She just grinned.

A lot of Hash names are like that, because it's traditional for Hashers to be named by the other members after completing a five-hash virgin period. Many of those names turn out to be rude, lewd and unprintable. Hashers also sing a lot. "Mostly rugby songs," said Pink Panther.

Beer Soup For the Hasher's Soles

In an age when people tend to take themselves (and everything around them) so seriously, it was refreshing to see an activity built around frivolity, foolishness and the tearing down of egos. You have to be pretty secure to run down Old Forest Road in a red dress - and I'm not even talking about the men.

"We got a lot of looks," said Susan Walton, one of Sunday's Hashers, "and at least one 'Faggot'!"

Meanwhile, Richard Morrison and Pink Panther had a little mishap. "I bent over to lay down a marker," said Panther, "and Richard ran over me, I guess he didn't see me. The problem was, I lost my wig, which was really embarrassing."

After the run the fifty-five Hashers gathered at Morrison's house where they drank beer, handed out awards and abused each other. The title of "Best Dressed" came down to Frank McPhatter in his hoop skirt, and Gopher, who drove down from Fort Eustis in a short wine-red cocktail dress set off with a gold necklace and matching hoop earrings - and a mustache.

"Interesting," said one of the bystanders. "A choice between the traditional, and the tacky."

Gopher, who got his dress off the rack at a Salvation Army store and his size-thirteen women's shoes from PayLess, got the nod. But the loser took it well.

"Can someone just help me get out of this thing?" he asked plaintively.

This article originally appeared in *The News & Advance* on February 12, 1997.

115

HASH FACT

Upon reaching 1000 runs with the one club, some Australian Hashers are granted a knighthood. This means that blokes you have known for ten years as 'Dickhead' and 'Tight Arse' suddenly became 'Sir Dickhead' and 'Sir Tight Arse.'

RUNNIN' THROUGH THE SHIGGY

Tom Dougherty

A Virgin Hasher gets his first taste of shiggy and learns that if you ain't bleeding, you ain't Hashing!

"ON-ON!" Damn those Hares. "RU?" Checking, Checking...

What the hell am I talking about? The Hockessin Hash House Harriers. If you wanna run with the pack, you gotta work the lingo, and these dudes meet about once a week to run, run, run for fun, fun, fun. The complex system of terms and phrases that you see above are used in their non-competitive runs called Hashes. Doing Hash runs and drinking afterwards is a centuries-old way to blow off steam, and there are Hashers all over the country. Some are trained runners, some are not. The one-year-old Hockessin group consists of corporate execs, military folk, tradespeople, and now, me. Their Hashing names are Up Chuck, Trisexual, Do Me, Fungi, Ass Wipe, Cumalot, Erection, and the fearless leader, Crib Snatcher, to name a few. And boy do people stare when they see this funky crew comin' down their street yelling out each other's names. "The Hash, if nothing else, is irreverent," says Crib Snatcher. I guess it adds to the experience - their hotline number is 302-NEEDFUN, and running, yelling, drinking and being vulgar, as we all know, will release a lot of that pent-up aggression and anxiety.

The day's events began with an explanation of the trail markings, mostly for the benefit of the virgins (myself and one other person on this particular day). The thing most stressed was that there are no rules, but you still need to know what you're doing, I guess. Basically, the running trail is always laid out in advance by 1-3 "Hares" who mark a cross-country course with "hashmarks" (splotches of flour). It began in Fungi's front yard, on your typical suburban street. We, the Hounds (about thirty runners strong), set out down the road, and someone sounded his bugle and cried "ON-ON!" ("I'm on the trail"). We soon came upon our first "X" mark, or check. This means that the trail can split off in several directions, and the Hounds must find the one true trail on which to proceed. The standard cry of "CHECKING" went up at this point, so Crib Snatcher and I decided to try running up a nearby steep hill - only to find a big fat "F" mark a few hashmarks later, indicating that we were on a false trail. The Hares are worthless scum, of course, and we were cursing them already.

Fortunately the FRB's, or Front Running Bastards (People who can actually run and tend to stay in the lead) had found the true trail and cried "ON-ON!" Clutching my asthma inhaler with one hand, and my heaving chest with the other, I thought of all the cigarettes I'd been smoking and tried to remember the last time I had exercised. As we headed back downhill towards the correct trail, I heard a nearby Hasher say, "Good lead, Crib Snatcher," referring to our useless run up the big hill.

Into the woods now, we wove through the polluted

streams and drainage ditches of suburbia, eventually passing under Kirkwood Highway. The creek became unavoidable, and most just took the pain and hopped in with both sneakers. Like a fool I had donned some fairly new footwear that morning, expecting neatly groomed trails and such. So, hopping from rock to rock to avoid the water, I soon found myself just about bringing up the rear, shouting "RU?" (are you on trail?) all the while. Back on the street, we passed an unusual trail marker consisting of a road-killed rabbit perfectly outlined with white flour. I thought of the Hares.

I was feeling better, warmed up to running, by the time we got to halfway point and a stop for a quick beer at someone's house. The worst was yet to come, but I was having a good time nonetheless. Back on the road we followed the white marks into a small causeway, the floor of which was coated with a half inch of water and the slipperiest green slime you can imagine. The crew didn't even bat an eye though, and we proceeded over hill and dale, on pavement, and through water.

"RU?"

"ON-ON!"

We entered on empty field, and the group scattered in all directions, searching. The trail could be anywhere. Experience is definitely a plus in this sport and, no thanks to me as usual, we finally found the trail leading up a steep embankment from the bed of a creek. This was the worst "shiggy" we got into that day, meaning thick underbrush. Judging by the assorted cuts, scrapes and gouges in Crib Snatcher's shins from an earlier Hash, I knew this was nothing. The hill was coated with an unearthly black muck that sort of resembled mud, and this time my shoes bought the farm. The gang helped each other get through the obstacles once again, and we were out.

After a quick jog through a neighborhood later, we arrived at the van for the ride home. Total elapsed time was about an hour and a half. We didn't go to the pub as I had expected, but there was a big picnic in Fungi's backyard. Then the rituals began. Everyone started singing and I didn't know what was going on, except that I had a DOWN-DOWN coming to me, since it was my first Hash. Crib Snatcher poured me a cold Rolling Rock, which I had to chug (DOWN-DOWN) in one try or wear the rest on my head. I sucked it down, and the rest is history.

This article originally appeared in the May 1996 Sports Issue of *Big Shout* Magazine.

HASH FACT

"Hair of the Dog" is, of course, a drink taken early in the morning to ease the pain of a hangover. "The *Hare* of the Dog" is the Hash version, referring to weekend trips where there might be a short run on the morning after the main event.

BEER RUNNERS
Oh, the Places They'll Go!

Christopher Rose

Six days a week, it is appropriate to accord the 150 members of the Hash House Harriers running club the perfunctory courtesies and respect worthy of others like them - workaday accountants, lawyers, welders, therapists, secretaries, office managers, whatever.

However on Monday nights the veneer of respectability is dashed as these people - Hashers, they call themselves - descend into their weekly ritual of pranksterism. They become a menace to society, a danger to democracy, a threat to pets, small children, golfers, shopping center security guards and railroad engineers. They become post-adolescent fraternity doofuses, spitball artists and class clowns with their silly songs and disruptive traditions, public vulgarities and secret nicknames.

But, despite their proclivities toward cross-dressing and the alarming frequency with which they contract poison ivy, they sure are a fun-loving bunch.

The New Orleans Hash House Harriers are the local branch of an international running organization that prioritizes pranksterism and partying over any real hint of fitness and competition.

They call themselves the "drinking club with a running

problem" and this does not seem inaccurate by any means. Unless the weekly run calls for costumes in keeping with occasional themed events (the annual bondage run, for instance, or this week's red dress run) the Hash House Harriers often resemble any other social running club - except there's more beer.

Once the weekly "race" begins, however, everything is different. An advance team of runners (called Hares) lays a trail of white flour for other runners (Hounds - get it?) to follow. Depending on the whims of the Hares, the run may follow a conventional roadside route or, more likely, will detour through public squares, parking ramps and dense woods - hence, the poison ivy - with many false trails along the way. (Once, when the trail led through the columned sidewalk corridor of the River Market shopping center on Tchoupitoulas street, security guards surrounded the bunch and made them sweep up their flour. "It was the most embarrassing moment in the history of the New Orleans club," says veteran hasher Chip Marz. "I've never heard of Hashers *anywhere* cleaning up their own flour!")

Anything goes. The run moves from one end of the area to the other, from the West Bank to Harahan to eastern New Orleans to downtown. Trails are marked from one beer stop to the next and the runners usually call it a day after four or five miles or so. Then they sing songs, welcome guests, initiate new members, all of which involves - you guessed it - drinking beer.

"We like to be seen, to cause a ruckus," says New Orleans Hasher Peter Caddoo, the club's current Grand Master and a beermaker for Dixie brewery. "We like to run through hotel lobbies and through shopping centers. We sometimes run on private property, but you shouldn't print that. Oh, go ahead and print it – we're never there very long anyway. We try to stay off golf courses because that would be disrupting a sporting event." (Within two hours of this statement, the Hash House Harriers pattered in general disarray between the 5th green and 11th fairway of Audubon Golf Course, disrupting all manner of genteel sporting life, but how could Caddoo have anticipated this? After all, he was a Hound, not a Hare.)

"I think most people here would tell you they run the Hash as a means of shedding stress," says Marz, who joined the New Orleans group only weeks after it formed back in 1988 and has run weekly ever since. "There's a lot of running groups that drink beer, but there's not a lot of running groups that go the places we go - places where runners don't usually go."

"A lot of people will come out and try this out for a night and decide it's not their cup of tea, and that's okay. But me, I first hashed in Jakarta, Indonesia in 1973, and it was love at first sight - running through rice fields, yelling and laughing. It's a good way to thumb your nose at society."

The Hash House Harriers were first formed by a group of British expatriates stationed in what is now called Malaysia. There have been dozens of international and local mutations over the years, but the call-and-response ("On! On!" and other cheers) and general methodology have remained intact: A wide communication network open to anybody foolish enough to join with lots of dirty songs, pornographic nicknames and, yep... beer.

There are more than 1,300 Hashes listed worldwide in at least 147 countries. Hashers who travel from one town to another usually can find a local group and if there isn't one, they often start one. The New Orleans chapter was started by the Houston club in October 1988, after it realized its southern sister city was without Hashers.

And one thing leads to another.

There are about 150 active members in the New Orleans club, all ages, all walks of life. The club serves a purpose far beyond its original mission, it seems.

"I got into it as an alternative to the bar scene," says local Grand Mistress Linda Crozier, a chemical sales representative. "You can meet a lot of interesting people out here."

Indeed. She met her husband in the group and then, after a real wedding, was host of a Hash wedding in Audubon Park for which all the guests cross-dressed.

"I had been in a number of other social running clubs and I had heard about how offensive these people were," says another local hasher, a 42-year-old women who asked that her real name not be used because she is a school teacher and fears what her supervisors might make of her Hasher membership.

"And, in fact, they *are* offensive," she continues. "Very unprofessional, but it's a wonderful opportunity to let your hair down, to laugh and sing and tell dirty jokes. It is idiotic, but fun." She pauses. "Although the poison ivy is a drawback."

Ryun Mouton first Hashed in Okinawa, Japan when he was in the Marines. "It was a great way to meet Japanese people and to see parts of Okinawa that I likely would never have seen," Mouton said.

His Hashing experiences there included rappelling down a mountainside and crawling through a tiny opening underneath a highway.

Mouton is a huge fan of Hashing, making road trips monthly to other cities and other states for "Interhashes" and other global events. He's done dozens of Hashes in many places in many styles and, as an authority on such matters, is able to distinguish the New Orleans Hash House Harriers from most other groups around the world. "More beer," he says.

This story originally appeared in *The Times-Picayune* on August 22, 1998.

HASH FACT

Hashspace is a kind of Facebook just for Hashers, where you can post your profile and photos, take part in blogs, form groups and generally give life meaning until the next Hash run.

HASH SONGS

While there are hundreds more songs out there, this "Mini-Hymnal" contains the standards which are sung at most Hashes.

HERE'S TO _____
(BASIC DOWN-DOWN SONG)

Here's to _____,

He's true blue,

He's a Hasher,

Through and through,

He's an asshole

So they say,

Tried to go to heaven,

But he went the other way,

So drink it down, down, down . . .

AUTOHASH SONG

Melody:" Oh Lord, Won't You Buy Me a Mercedes-Benz?"

This one is for those who choose to drive, rather than run.

(International version)

Dear Lord, won't you give me a ride to the beer,
My friends are all drinking, and I'm stuck out here,
I'll ride in a lorry, rickshaw, or tuk tuk,
If you drive me there, I'll throw in a down, down, down...

(USA version)

Dear Lord, won't you give me a ride to the beer,
My friends are all drinking, and I'm stuck out here,
I'll ride in a Chevy, a Ford or a truck,
If you drive me there. I'll throw in a down, down, down...

129

THE BEERY BUNCH

Melody: "Brady Bunch Theme"

Here's the story,
Of a thirsty Hasher,
Who was running at the back of the pack.
Every bad trail that there was,
Well he found it.
He must have run for miles!

It's the story,
Of some sacred nectar,
That was chilling with a mind of its own.
It was one beer,
Sitting in the cooler,
Yet it still had no foam.

'Till the circle,
When the Hasher met the nectar.
And he knew it just couldn't stick around.
That's when his shorts went down around his ankles,
And the beer became a down down down down down!

A down down down!
A down down down!
That's the waaaaayyyyyyy it became a down down down!

BIRTHDAY SONG

Melody: "Happy Birthday To You"

Happy birthday, fuck you,

Happy birthday, fuck you,

Happy birthday, you asshole,

Happy birthday, fuck you.

Drink it down, down, down . . .

HER LEFT TIT

Melody: "My Bonnie Lies Over the Ocean"

Her left tit hangs down to her belly,
Her right tit hangs down to her knee.
If her left tit did equal her right tit,
She'd get lots of weenie from me.
Drink it down, down, down . . .

HE'S THE MEANEST

He's the meanest,
He sucks the horse's penis,
He's the meanest,
He's a horse's ass.

Ever since he found it,
All he does is pound it,
He's the meanest,
He's a horse's ass.

He's always pissing on us,
He's rotten and dishonest,
He's the meanest,
He's a horse's ass.
So drink it down, down, down . . .

HE WANKS HIS CRANK

He wanks his crank in the morning,
He wanks his crank in the night,
He wanks his crank with his left hand,
And he cleans it up with his right.

So drink it down, down, down . . .

FORESKIN SONG

Melody: "My Bonnie Lies Over the Ocean"

My one skin hangs down to my two skin,
My two skin hangs down to my three,
My three skin hangs down to my foreskin,
My foreskin hangs down to my knees.

Roll back, roll back,
Roll back my foreskin for me, for me.
Roll back, roll back,
Please roll back my foreskin for me.
Drink it down, down, down . . .

IF YOUR GIRLFRIEND TASTES LIKE SHIT

Melody: "If You're Happy and You Know It"

If your girlfriend tastes like shit, turn her over,
If your girlfriend tastes like shit, turn her over,
If your girlfriend tastes like shit,
It's her asshole not her clit,
If your girlfriend tastes like shit, turn her over!

IT'S A SMALL DICK

Melody: "It's a Small World"

Well it isn't long and it isn't thick,
It gets hard too slow and it cums too quick,
It gets lost in her twat,
But it's all that he's got,
It's a small, small, dick.

It's a small dick after all,
It's a small dick after all,
Always limp from alcohol,
It's a small, small, dick!

MEET THE HASHERS

Melody: "Flintstones Theme"

Hashers, meet the Hashers,

They're the biggest drunks in history.

From the town of _____,

They're the leaders in debauchery.

Half minds, trailing shiggy through the years,

Watch them as they down a lot of beers,

Down down, down down down down,

Down down down down down down down down down,

Down down, down down down down,

Down down down down down down down down down.

SOLDIER SONG

Ass-hole, ass-hole, a soldier I will be,

To piss, to piss, two pistols on my knee,

For cunt, for cunt, for country and for king,

Asshole, asshole, asshole, asshole,

A soldier I will be.

Drink it down, down, down . . .

THERE WAS A LITTLE BIRD

There was a little bird,
No bigger than a turd,
Sitting on a telephone pole.
He ruffled up his neck,
And shit about a peck,
And puckered up his little asshole,
Asshole, asshole, asshole,
He puckered up his little asshole.

THEY OUGHT TO BE PISSED ON

Melody: "My Bonnie Lies Over the Ocean"

They ought to be publicly pissed on,
They ought to be publicly shot (bang, bang!),
They ought to be tied to a urinal,
And left there to fester and rot.
Drink it down, down, down . . .

WHERE WERE YOU LAST WEEK?

Melody: "Where, Oh Where, Are You Tonight?" (Hee Haw)

Note: This tune is used to serenade Hashers who have not come to the Hash in awhile...

Where, oh where, were you last week?
Why did you make us Hash all alone?
You fat lazy bastards,
You weren't even here.
So we fucked all the virgins,
And drank all the beer!

Drink it down, down, down, down . . .

WHY ARE WE WAITING?

Melody: "Come Let Us Adore Him"

Note: This tune is used to encourage Hashers who are taking too long to complete a down-down...

Why are we waiting,
Could be fornicating (or masturbating),
Oh, why are we waiting,
So fucking long, etc...

WHY WAS HE BORN SO BEAUTIFUL?

Why was he born so beautiful?
Why was he born at all?
He's no fuckin' use to anyone,
He's no fuckin' use at all.
They say he's a joy to his mother,
But he's a pain in the asshole to me.

So drink it down, down, down . . .

ZICKY-ZACKY

The purpose of the zicky-zacky chant is to point out breaches in circle etiquette - members of the circle surround the offender, point with their elbows, and repeat this chant loudly:

Zicky-zacky, zicky-zacky,

Hoy, Hoy, Hoy!

Zicky-zacky, zicky-zacky,

Hoy, Hoy, Hoy!

Zicky-zacky, zicky-zacky,

Hoy, Hoy, Hoy!

...........and so on, until offender completes a down-down. Alternatively, the zicky-zacky chant can be performed whenever someone screws up a verse in a Hash song (of course, the offending singer must immediately do a down-down while the pack chants).

CLOSE TO BREW

Melody: "Close to You"

Why do Hashers suddenly appear,
Every time, beer is near?
Just like me,
They long to be,
Close to brew.
Ahhhhh Ahhhh Ahh,
Close to brew.
Ahhhhh Ahhhh Ahh,
Down Down Down!

YOU AIN'T NOTHIN' BUT A HASHER
Melody: "You Ain't Nothin' But A Hound Dog"

You ain't nothin' but a Hasher,
A-humpin' all the time,
You ain't nothin' but a Hasher,
A-humpin' all the time.
You ain't never caught a Hare,
And you ain't no friend of mine.

BITCH A DOG

Melody: "Do, Re, Mi" (Sound of Music)

Bitch, a dog, a female dog,
Itch, a place for you to scratch,
Hitch, I pull my knickers up,
Grab, another word for snatch,
Bath, a place for making gin,
Sex, another word for sin,
Prick, a needle going in,
And that will bring us back to
Bitch, bitch, bitch, bitch . . .

FURBURGER KING

Melody: "Burger King Jingle"

Hold my pickle, I'll eat your lettuce,

Cunnilingus don't upset us,

All we ask is that you let us,

Have it your way.

Have it your way - sit on my face,

Have it your way - give us a taste,

Have it your way… at Furburger King.

(I WANT A) GANG BANG

Melody: "Ta-Ra-Ra, Boom-D-A"

I want a gang bang *if* I could,

Because a gang bang *feels* so good.

When I was young and *in* my prime,

I used to gang bang *all* the time.

But now I'm old and *getting* gray,

And only gang bang *once* a day.

So I just *have* to say,

Let's gang bang *anyway!*

RAWHIDE

Melody: "Rawhide"

Rollin', rollin', rollin',
My dick is getting' swollen,
I got this doggie rollin', Rawhide.

My knob is hard as leather,
But I'll get it in whatever,
I wish I could get the tip inside,

I stab but I keep missin',
This wasn't made for pissin',
I'm waiting for this year's first ride.

CHORUS:
Pull 'em down, get 'em off,
Get 'em off, pull 'em down,
Pull 'em down, Get 'em off, Rawhide.
Stick it in, pull it out,
Pull it out, stick it in,
Stick it in, pull it out, Rawhide.

She's movin', movin', movin',
Stops my manhood groovin',
This doggie won't stop movin', Rawhide.

Beer Soup For the Hasher's Soles

It's gonna be sore later,
But I've been a masturbator,
All those years that I've just spent inside,

My balls, they are aching,
From years of wanking and waiting,
Waiting to get this thing inside.

Rollin', rollin', rollin',
I'm rootin' her assholin',
We're mounted doggy style, Rawhide.

I don't try to understand her,
Just catch and grope and bang her,
Now her twat is getting' wet and wide,

My foreskin's torn and tattered,
Her pussy's worn and battered,
At last I'll drop my load inside.

Rawwwww…. hide!

TAKE ME OUT TO THE GANG BANG

Melody: "Take Me Out to the Ball Game"

Take me out to the Gang Bang,

I like sex with a crowd,

Three-somes and four-somes are truly grand,

Use your tongue, your dick, or a hand,

'Cuz it's shoot, shoot, shoot all your hot cream,

If you don't cum, it's a shame,

For it's one, two,

She's covered in goo,

At the Ol' Gang Bang!

YANKEE DOODLE

Melody: "I'm a Yankee Doodle Dandy"

Yank my doodle it's a dandy,
Yank my doodle till I die,
Make that wiener shoot some fireworks,
Just like the Fourth of July.

I've got a Yankee Doodle boner,
I've had it since you rubbed my thigh,
So yank my doodle if you please.
That bulge is not a pony,
Yank my doodle till I die . . .

DOUGH, RAY, ME

Melody: "Do, Re, Mi" (Sound of Music)

Dough, the stuff, that buys me beer,

Ray, the guy who serves me beer,

Me, the guy, who drinks the beer,

Far, a long way to the john,

So, I'll have another beer,

La, I'll have another beer,

Tea, no thanks I'll have a beer,

And that brings us back to,

Dough . . . (etc)

155

BALL GAME

Melody: "Take Me Out to the Ball Game"

Whip it out at the ball game,

Wave it round at the crowd,

Dip it in Jello and Crackerjacks,

I don't care if you give it a whack,

Because it's beat your meat at the ball game,

If you don't come it's a shame,

For it's one, two,

And you're covered in goo,

At the old ball game!

SWILLIGAN'S ISLAND

Melody: "Gilligan's Island Theme"

Just sip yer brew and you'll hear a tale,
A tale of a drunken Hash.
That started with a keg of beer,
And everyone got trashed. (Repeat)

The first Hare was a brainless cooch,
His co-Hare was half as smart.
Two hundred some odd half-minds,
Took off in a cloud of farts. (Repeat)

The hills got steep, the shiggy deep,
The back checks had them fooled.
Then someone found the beer stop,
And everybody drooled. (Repeat)

The mud had sucked their sneakers off,
Their legs were ripped a lot.
But once they had their nectar,
The trail they soon forgot. (Repeat)

The moral is no matter how,
Much shiggy's on your trail,
A Hashin' twit don't give a shit,
While he's swilling his cold ale.

THE HASH HOUSE HARRIERS

Melody: "The Addams Family Theme"

Their drinking is compulsive,
Their running is convulsive,
They're morally repulsive,
The Hash House Harriers!

CHORUS:
Da da da da (snap fingers twice)
Da da da da (snap fingers twice)
Da da da da, da da da da, da da da da

Their flatulance is rude and,
Their genitals protrude when,
They're running in the nude in,
The Hash House Harriers!

CHORUS:
Da da da da (snap fingers twice)
Da da da da (snap fingers twice)
Da da da da, da da da da, da da da da

They're always shiggy-tracking
From constantly bushwhacking.
Intelligence they're lacking.
The Hash House Harriers!

Duh-duh-duh-duh... down-down
Duh-duh-duh-duh... down-down
Duh-duh-duh-duh... Duh-duh-duh-duh...
Duh-duh-duh-duh... down-down!

HOLIDAY SONGS

Hashers are a merry bunch to be sure, and seize every opportunity to spread... uh... er... holiday cheer!

CHIPMUNKS ROASTING ON AN OPEN FIRE

Melody: "The Christmas Song" (Nat King Cole)

Chipmunks roasting on an open fire,

Jack Frost ripping up your nose,

Yuletide carolers being thrown in the fire,

And folks dressed up like buffaloes.

Everybody knows a turkey slaughtered in the snow,

Helps to make the season right,

Tiny tots with their eyes all gouged out,

Will find it hard to see tonight.

They know that Santa's on his way,

He's loaded lots of guns and bullets on his sleigh,

And every mother's child is sure to spy,

To see if reindeer really scream when they die.

And so I'm offering this simple phrase,

To kids from one to ninety-two,

Although it's been said many times, many ways,

Merry Christmas,

Merry Christmas,

Merry Christmas,

Screw you.

EDDIE THE HORNY REINDEER

Melody: "Rudolph the Red-Nosed Reindeer"

Eddie the horny reindeer,
Used to love the reindeer snatch.
You would always find him looking,
Searchin' every bush and thatch.

All of the other reindeer,
Used to love to get a lay.
But Eddie the horny reindeer,
Had to have it every day.

Then one foggy Christmas Eve,
Santa came to say,
"Sorry Ed to be so blunt,
But if you don't eat pussy, you'll get no cunt."

Now all the reindeer love him,
And you'll hear them shout with glee.
"Eddie the horny reindeer,
Won't you please go down on me?"

HOLIDAY SONG

Melody: "Let it Snow"

Well, the weather outside is frightful,

But my dick is so delightful,

If you really want to see it grow,

Give it a blow, give it a blow, give it a blow.

IT'S BEGINNING TO LOOK A LOT LIKE SYPHILIS

Melody: "It's Beginning to Look a Lot Like Christmas"

It's beginning to look a lot like syphilis,
It's the holiday drip!
Take a look at the purple sores,
Rotting through to the core,
Of the blue veins, on your candy cane,
Of love!

It's beginning to look a lot like syphilis,
It stings, when I pee.
My brain has turned to purple,
And my sperm has begun to curdle,
My dick looks funny, it's green and runny,
With fleas!

Beer Soup For the Hasher's Soles

CHORUS SONGS

ALOUETTE

Melody: "Alouette"

Note: This tune requires an unsuspecting female volunteer.

CHORUS:

Alouette, gentille Alouette,
Alouette je te plumerai.

Leader: Does she have ze stringy hair?
All: Oui, she has ze stringy hair.
Leader: Stringy hair,
All: Stringy hair,
Leader: Alouette! Aah, aah, aah, aah . . . (chorus)

Leader: Does she have ze furrowed brow?
All: Oui, she has ze furrowed brow,
Leader: Furrowed brow,
All: Furrowed brow,
Leader: Stringy hair,
All: Stringy hair,
Leader: Alouette! Aah, aah, aah, ahh . . . (chorus)

Wooden eye (Yes I would!) . . .
Broken nose . . .
Blow job lips . . .
Two buck teeth . . .
Double chin . . .
Swinging tits . . .
Beer belly . . .
Bulbous butt . . .
Furry thing . . .

Leader: Now isn't she a nice-a girl?
All: Oui, she is a nice-a girl,
Leader: Nice-a girl,
All: Nice-a girl,
Leader: Alouette! Aah, aah, aah . . .

Chorus

Leader/All: How I love her (repeat all)

YOGI BEAR SONG

Melody: "Camptown Races"

Note: Take turns leading verses

There is a bear in the deep dark woods,
Yogi, Yogi,
There is a bear in the deep dark woods,
Yogi, Yogi Bear.

CHORUS (REPEAT PREVIOUS VERSE):
Yogi, Yogi Bear,
Yogi, Yogi Bear,
There is a bear in the deep dark woods,
Yogi, Yogi Bear.

Other verses:

Yogi has a little friend, Boo-Boo, Boo-Boo Bear...
Boo-Boo has a girlfriend, Cyndi, Cyndi Bear...
Yogi has a girlfriend, Suzi, Suzi Bear...
Cyndi has a shaven snatch, Grizzly, Grizzly Bear...
Cyndi wears crotchless undies, Teddy, Teddy Bear...
Cyndi likes it on the ice, Polar, Polar Bear...
Cyndi isn't on the pill, Pregnant, Pregnant Bear...
Suzi likes it up the rear, Dirty, Dirty Bear...
Suzi's boyfriend has no teeth, Gummi, Gummi Bear...
Suzi's snatch it smells like cheese, Camel, Camel Bear...

Beer Soup For the Hasher's Soles

Suzi she has great big tits, More than, More than (I can bear)
Suzi gets four bits an hour, Jingle, Jingle...
Cyndi's tampon has no string, Cotton, Cotton...
Yogi didn't use a condom, Daddy, Daddy...
Boo-Boo likes it upside down, Koala, Koala....
Boo-Boo has a twelve-inch cock, Cindy's a lucky bear...
Boo-Boo's only three feet tall, Midget, Midget...
Boo-Boo likes it up the butt, Yogi's a lucky bear...
Yogi didn't wipe his butt, Brown, Brown...
Yogi uses Afro-Sheen, Black, Black...
Yogi got a case of crabs, Itchy, Itchy...
Yogi lights Kuwaiti farts, Saddam, Saddam...
Boo-Boo likes to stroke his tool, Wanker, Wanker...
Yogi also likes young boys, Poofter, Poofter...
Song ender: Yogi he has HIV, Dying, Dying . . .

BESTIALITY'S BEST

Melody: "Tie Me Kangaroo Down"

Take turns leading verses. This one requires a good memory, or at least enough wit to think of rhymes on the spot.

CHORUS:
Bestiality's best, boys,
Bestiality's best - FUCK A WALLABY!
Bestiality's best, boys,
Bestiality's best.

Change your luck with a duck, Chuck,
Change your luck with a duck,
A duck's a marvelous fuck, Chuck,
So change your luck with a duck. (chorus)

You can shoot your load in a toad, dude,
You can shoot your load in a toad,
If there's nothing else to be rode, dude,
You can shoot your load in a toad. (chorus)

You can come again in a hen, men,
You can come again in a hen,
When you've had everything else in the pen, men,
You can come again in a hen. (chorus)

You can try your log in a frog, boys,
You can try your log in a frog,
If it's the only thing in the bog, boys,
You can try your log in a frog. (chorus)

170

(Continue with following suggested verses)

Stick your dork in a stork…
Grind your mound on a hound…
Be a queer with a deer…
Chuck your sperm in a worm…
Get in deep with a sheep…
Stick your dick in a tick…
Give some cock to a croc…
Be a pimp for a chimp…
Get in the sack with yak…
Have intercourse with a horse…
Etc, etc……

THE S&M MAN
Melody: "The Candy Man"

Who can take a bicycle,
Take away the seat,
Put his girlfriend on it,
And ride down a bumpy street?

CHORUS:
It's the S&M man, oh the S&M man,
The S&M man because he mixes it with love,
And makes the hurt feel good.
The hurt feel good.

Who can take a golf club,
Shove it up her twat,
Move it back and forth,
'Til he locates her G-spot,
(CHORUS)
Who can take a hammer,
Wave it overhead,
And slam it on his pecker,
'Til he wishes he were dead?
(CHORUS)
Who can take sandpaper,
Gotta be fifty grit,
Rub it back and forth,
'Til she has a bleeding clit?

172

Who can take a razor,
And use no shaving cream,
Then scrape her pussy bald,
While he listens to her scream?
(CHORUS)
Who can take a chainsaw,
Cut the bitch in two,
Fuck the bottom half,
And toss the other half to you?
(CHORUS)
Who can take two ice picks,
Stick one in each ear,
And ride her like a Harley,
While he fucks her up the rear?
(CHORUS)
Who can take a Doberman,
Watch him do a show,
Let him fuck your girlfriend,
While he takes a video?
(CHORUS)
Who can take a puppy,
Hold it by the ears,
Fuck it in the ass,
Until it sheds those puppy tears?
(CHORUS)

INTERNATIONAL HASH HYMN
Melody: Swing Low, Sweet Chariot

Note: gestures accompany words!

Swing low, sweet chariot,
Coming for to carry me home,
Swing low, sweet chariot,
Coming for to carry me home.

I looked over Jordan and what did I see,
Coming for to carry me home,
A band of angels coming after me,
Coming for to carry me home.

If you get there before I do,
Coming for to carry me home,
Tell all my friends that I'm coming too,
Coming for to carry me home.

Swing low, sweet chariot,
Coming for to carry me home,
Swing low, sweet chariot,
Coming for to carry me home.

May the Hash go in peace!

HASH FACT

'Swing Low, Sweet Chariot' was written by Harry Thacker Burleigh (1866-1949) and has been universally adopted as the official Hash Hymn. Usually performed with various alternative versions (humming, Chinese, silent, Reggie etc). It is used to close the Hash Circle, and preceded by "Gentlemen of the Hash, Hats and pots on the floor." This tradition, although by no means universal, has been is taken up by numerous other hashes.

AUTHOR

"Humper" first began Hashing with the Wednesday Australian Capital Territory (WACT) Hash in Canberra Australia in 1994. He has since been a semi-regular with the Humpin' Hash in Oceanside, California and the Tampa and Jolly Roger Hashes in Florida, in addition to visiting other kennels whenever possible. He is now a "Hasher at Large," so you never know where he may turn up!

On Out!